'I met May Nicholson in a small flat with a group of inner city kids along with Jock Stein and Ian Maxwell. (May will never forget that I ate the last cookie!). May reached out to me with her directness and love of Jesus and won my heart in a moment! You will meet her here in Miracles from Mayhem *along with many of her family and friends. She will take you from the chaos of her broken community to the embracing love of Jesus. Her story will break your heart, renew your love, and hopefully give you a compassion for the poor.*

Years later, I heard May speak at a Scottish National Prayer Breakfast seminar, standing before Members of Parliament, lords and ladies, and other leaders from across the nation. Her first words of love and greeting that morning went to the women's cloakroom attendants whom she had invited to join us. As they stood on the fringes of the crowd she made them the centre of her love and care. That has been the story of her life ... loving Christ by caring for the broken outsider; putting people in the centre of life with the love of Jesus.

May has the same love for the poorest of the poor and the richest of the rich. She is at home with lords and ladies and with the lowly and loneliest. Living out God's love with and among the poor, she reflects Jesus who, "Though he was rich, yet for our sake he became poor that we might be made rich".'

Chuck Wright

'Anyone who has lived with drug addicts and alcoholics knows how elusive hope is. It runs through your fingers like fine sand, until there's nothing left but cynicism and despair. But May Nicholson found a different sort of hope – rather, it found her! Her encounter with Jesus Christ literally 'saved' her life, and set in motion what one of her colleagues

calls 'a friendly steamroller' - clearing paths of hope not just for herself but for dozens and dozens of others too.

This is the sort of story that could be labelled "unbelievable", except that it happens to be true! It's told honestly, with helpful angles from those whose lives interacted with May, and with an ever-present sympathy and understanding for all. Read it; study it in your churches to see what you can do; and give it to anyone who needs hope.'

John Nicholls,
London City Mission

'I have often referred to May Nicholson as "the Mother Theresa of Scotland", and this delightful book confirms that title. The key to May's amazing ministry is in her prayer after conversion: "I'd like to have millions and millions of Jesus' love so that wherever I go it will spill out on the people I meet." I have seen this love spill out on drug addicts and duchesses, politicians and prisoners in Dundee, Paisley, Northern Ireland and Romania. I can't wait to see what May does next!'

Louise S Purvis

Miracles from Mayhem

The story of May Nicholson

By Irene Howat

CHRISTIAN
FOCUS

Copyright © May Nicholson 2004

ISBN 978-1-85792-897-6

Published in 2004
Reprinted 2005, 2006, 2007, 2011 and 2017
by
Christian Focus Publications, Ltd.
Geanies House, Fearn, Ross-shire,
IV20 1TW, Scotland

www.christianfocus.com

Cover design by Moose77.com
Printed and bound by Nørhaven, Denmark

Contents

Foreword

by The Earl of Dundee

Some stories have to be written. May Nicholson's is one of them. It is compulsive reading. Yet the enduring impact is the message that you take away with you.

Firstly, there is the witness to the change in May's life. Not least is this provided by a doctor who met her both before and after her conversion. He writes, 'When I knew her previously May was a deeply depressed alcohol addict with no hope and her life was going nowhere. She seemed in utter chaos. Now May was completely and utterly different. The transformation in her life was dramatic and complete – yes, miraculous.' And it is this change that makes her so effective in helping people, as is evident from the account of her works in Paisley, Dundee and Glasgow.

Secondly, reflected in *Miracles from Mayhem* is an affirmation of the Christian gospel. On the theme of repentance from sin and newness of life, one of May's colleagues remarks that when asked about the slash marks on her arms she would reply, 'These are the marks of my old life, but the life I have now is the new one in Jesus.'

Thirdly, and above all, May's story rekindles our own belief in the God of miracles and his ability to enter the mayhem of daily life. 'I will restore to you the years the locusts have eaten' (Joel 2:25). May Nicholson thanks God for giving back to her all the years that were wasted with drink, drugs and self-harming.

Miracles in Mayhem will make you laugh and weep. It will not leave you unmoved. But while it will benefit all its readers, in particular it speaks to those who are in despair. For May's life demonstrates the most uplifting experience of any time and place, the replacement of hopelessness by confidence, love and joy.

Alexander Dundee
March 2004

1

Back to the Beginning

My old man's a dyer
He works in Coats' mill
He gets his pay on a Friday
And he buys half a gill.
He goes to church on a Sunday
A half an hour late
He pulls the buttons off his shirt
And puts them in the plate.

That song makes me smile. My dad sang it to me countless times and hundreds of other Paisley dads sang it to their children too. Coats' Mill was big business in the town when I was young and it was one of the major employers. Dad worked long hours and I used to watch at the window for him coming home. Mum would be rushing around to have his tea on the table almost as soon as he came in. It's changed days now. Some of the men I know come home and make the dinner. My dad wouldn't have known where to start!

My story doesn't begin there, of course, and I'd love to trace back my family history to find out more about it. But what I do know explains a lot about my childhood. Mum had a tragic background. Her parents came to Paisley from Ireland. Grandpa went away to the First World War and like millions of others he didn't come home again. The last Granny saw of him was when he put on his scratchy new soldier's uniform and marched proudly out to serve king and country. I can imagine how proud she felt as she watched him go, and I'm sure she kept her fears to herself. Granny must have been afraid because she had more than a dozen children and nothing to live on except her soldier husband's pay. When she was left a widow Granny decided to go with the children to New Zealand. But she changed her mind at the very last minute and marched them all away from the ship.

Mum's home was poor, and I mean really poor. As soon as she was able Mum went to work at the mill. I just hate the thought of her working there. Looms were huge clanking brutes of things. The weaver peddled a contraption that lifted the warp threads up and down as the shuttle shot from side to side with the weft. Weavers got into a rhythm as they worked and the one thing that disturbed the rhythm was a thread breaking. Young girls were employed to work below the looms and their job was to watch for threads breaking then to grab them and knot them together again so that the weaver didn't have to slow down or stop. Slowing down and stopping cost time and therefore money, and the overseers soon spotted when that happened and docked the weaver's wage. So these girls, some as young as eight or nine, couldn't let their concentration lapse for a minute or they would get a kick from the weaver or his overseer.

Just imagine what it was like for a girl like Mum. The noise was unbearable and she soon learned to lip-read. Even though she had a cloth wrapped round her mouth and nose and a scarf round her head the fine dust from the loom went everywhere. There can't have been a millgirl that didn't have dust in her lungs at the end of the day. And it was everywhere else too, all over her clothes, in her hair and ears, trapped under her fingernails. And that was when things were going well. Sometimes a girl needed a kick to tell her that a thread had broken, because even if the weaver screamed at her he wouldn't have been heard, and if she jumped she was in danger of having her hair caught in the loom. Some girls were killed under the looms. It was a dangerous as well as a horrible job. But it had to be done; and my granny needed the money.

There was a school for mill children but it cost a penny to attend. As Granny needed every penny to feed and clothe her children Mum wasn't able to go. A farthing was a lot of money to Granny and a penny for education was too much to pay. I think it made Mum sad that she had very little education for she was a clever and able woman and could have made something of it. The first time Dad took Mum home to meet his family she must have felt as though she was entering a different world. It was probably the first time she held a china cup and saucer. I imagine she was scared stiff she would drop them!

Every Sunday we visited Dad's parents. We went in, sat down and never moved. My brothers and sisters and I watched Granny arrange the cups and saucers and side plates. Side plates! We thought we were visiting millionaires! The children weren't allowed to sit at the table and we had to watch the grown-ups having their tea before we had any. I still remember watching a cake, never taking my eyes off it and wishing that nobody would choose that one. And I can still feel the disappointment like a punch in the stomach when somebody did. Dad's mother always had plenty of food on the table but Mum warned us within an inch of our lives not to take more than one thing. Occasionally, on the walk over to our Sunday visit, our hearts sank when Mum told us that we weren't to eat anything at all. When Granny offered us a cake or biscuit we had to grin and say, 'No thank you. I'm not hungry.' Sometimes Mum had a need to show her in-laws that her children weren't hungry, even when we were. There were many nights I went to bed with my stomach rumbling with hunger and Mum's words of wisdom ringing in my ears like cold comfort. 'Away to sleep,' she'd tell us. 'That'll make the morning come quicker and there's bread for the morning.'

I loved my Dad's father. He used to tell us such good stories, stories we wanted to believe but never knew if they were true or not. All these years later I can still hear his voice telling me one of them. 'I was on the top deck of a tram,' he said, 'when this man in a business suit came on and told me I'd stolen his watch! Do you think I'd do a thing like that, May?' I shook my head, and said I didn't. I'd heard the story so often, but that didn't make me want him to hurry it. It was so good. With a sigh of contentment I relaxed on his knee and let him get on with it. 'Well, I told the man that I'd not stolen his watch at all. "Yes, you did!" he shouted. "No, I didn't," said I. "Yes, you did!" "I did not!" Then the police arrived on the scene and climbed up the stairs of the tram.' By now I was holding my breath. "You've lost a watch?" the policeman asked, and the businessman admitted that he had. "Well," said the policeman, "we found it in the toilet." The businessman was so embarrassed that he offered to give me £5. 'Did I take it, May?' he would ask. 'No, you didn't take it,' I replied. How I loved this game! 'Then he offered me £20, May, enough to buy a wee flat in a tenement. Did I take it?' 'No, Grandpa, you didn't take it,' said I. 'Then what happened? He offered me £50, enough to buy a beautiful bungalow.' The whole family was listening now, waiting for the punch line. "Done!" I said, and the businessman took out his wallet and started to count the pound notes. "One, two, three, four, five", Grandpa counted slowly and I joined in, my voice rising with excitement when he got to the mid-forties. "'Forty- six, forty-seven, forty-eight, forty-nine ..." Then, out of the blue I heard your granny shouting, "Hoi, Hughie! Come on Hughie, it's time to get up or you'll be late for your work!"' It was ages before I worked out that was a joke, and even then I loved when he told me it.

Granny sat like a queen reigning when we visited. When I think back I know she was queen of a very small country as they just had a wee house. But there seemed so much room in it because there were just the two of them. In our home there was nearly a dozen of us and there were no side plates, in fact, sometimes we drank our tea from jam jars. There were enough dishes to go round until something was broken then one of us had to wait for someone to finish their meal before he got his. Mum's mother died before I was born but I feel I can remember Granny because Mum spoke a lot about her.

I was born in Ferguslie Park in Paisley in a traditional room and kitchen with a tiny WC on the landing. The room had a built-in bed, complete with curtains to give some privacy. All of us were born in that bed and the biggest luxury we could have was to be sick and cuddled up in the built-in bed. When I was three or four years old we moved to a brand new house in Ferguslie Park, the biggest council housing scheme in Europe at the time. Our new home had two bedrooms, a kitchen and – wonder of wonders – our very own bathroom! It was pure luxury. Mum's brother John, and his wife Lizzie, lived right next door with her seventeen children. And we didn't even have to go outside to see them. Instead we opened a hatch in the hall, hopped down into the darkness, felt our way along to the corresponding hatch in Aunt Lizzie's house, and knocked on it until one of our cousins opened it and let us in. It was like a rat run for the children of both families. Sometimes we frightened the wits out of other neighbours by banging on the underside of their hatches with a brush handle! Apart from that the worst mischief we got into was knocking on peoples' doors and running away before they were answered. Of course, we could only do that when the evenings were dark. At the end of our road was a part of Ferguslie Park that was kept for 'undesirables'. People actually called the area 'The Undesirables'. Council officials did regular checks to see that the people there were looking after their houses. If any of them had ever come into our house they would have discovered it spotlessly clean. We were poor but we were clean.

Aunt Lizzie's family next door were our closest friends as well as our relations and we saw a lot of them. Other members of the extended family lived differently from us. In fact, when we went to visit one aunt she put newspapers on the floor to stop us messing up her linoleum. She was the only person we knew who had a television set but we weren't allowed to watch it. But who needed television when we had all our toys to play with? Dad made us stilts out of National Dried Milk tins by punching holes on either side of them and threading string through the holes. We were measured to make sure the string reached up to our hands, then it was knotted inside the tin. With our new toys we thought we were just great as we clomped up and down the street. Then there were our skipping ropes made out of old bits of washing line. Given an old length of rope the fun was endless. We skipped on our own, in twos with a longer rope and in twos with one end tied to a lamppost. And if there was a crowd of us we skipped in turns while two girls 'ca'ed' the ends of the rope.

Dolls were among my favourite toys and I made my own from clothes pegs. Nowadays you can spend good money buying clothes peg doll kits. My mother would have given herself a pain laughing if she'd ever seen one of them. I drew a face on the clothes pegs and either drew hair or stuck on bits of string. Then I made them dresses out of whatever I could get. Even rags were hard to come by because the ragman came round the streets buying rags in exchange for cups. My peg dolls looked good in clothes made of paper too. When I was ten or eleven I was given a real doll and I thought heaven had come on earth.

Birthdays weren't celebrated but Christmas certainly was. We hung up our socks and were thrilled with the bits and pieces we found in them the next morning. They always included a tangerine and a silver threepenny piece. And that wasn't all. One year we got a cardboard sweet shop that kept us in fun for months. Another year a cardboard post office complete with paper pound notes and cardboard coins arrived at Christmas. We could not have been better pleased even if the pound notes had been real and the coins made of silver. When the cardboard toys eventually gave up the ghost we had our imaginations to fall back on. Playing 'wee houses' gave us endless pleasure. With pebbles for potatoes, dock seeds for tea, dandelion leaves for vegetables and bits of paper wrapped in twists for sweets we were all the way there for a good afternoon's play. And in summer, when the nights were long and light, we put on concerts in the back greens and performed to audiences from up and down the street.

I love seeing my grandchildren with all their nice toys but I didn't feel deprived when I was a girl because I didn't have any. The thing about being poor in Ferguslie Park in the 1950s was that everyone was just the same as we were. We didn't know we were poor because nobody thought to tell us. And even some famous pop singers of the day must have been poor too. I remember Lonnie Donnigan singing, 'My old man's a dustman; he wears a dustman's hat. He wears "Cor blimey" trousers and he lives in a council flat.' We were like the pop singer; we lived in a council flat. It never occurred to me that Lonnie Donnigan's dad might not! Maybe his dad was better off and sometimes bought him sweets. They were an absolute luxury in our house. But down the road there was a man who used to organise races for us, but only when he was drunk. I used to watch for him coming to see if he was unsteady on his feet before running down to meet him. He'd line us up according to our ages, 'Ready, steady, go!' and we were off, pelting down the street as though our lives depended on it. There was a lot at stake because the older winners got a shilling for sweets and the younger ones were given a sixpence. I ran like a hare to win the money but I would never have bought sweets with it. Sixpence or a shilling would put such a smile on Mum's face and that made not buying sweets all worthwhile. The poor man must have wondered where his money had gone when he woke up sober the next morning. Very occasionally Granny gave me a two-shilling piece. When that happened my feet had wings as I careered down road after road back to Ferguslie Park to give Mum a fortune. 'That's God's gift to keep us till pay day', she would say, and even as a girl I could feel her relief.

Dad wasn't always as careful with money, which was why he felt able to buy a greyhound. No doubt he argued that it would keep itself on its winnings at the greyhound races, but all I knew was that the dog seemed to get better food than we did sometimes. And he had a kennel all to himself in the back green. For all our poverty we did have our little luxuries. Mum did the washing in a boiler in the washhouse. The water was heated up for the washing then cooled down for us children. Ah, the luxury of the deep warm soapy water. Mind you, it wasn't clean when the first of us went into it and it certainly wasn't clean by the time the last of us climbed out!

Everyone moved into the housing scheme at the same time and none of the families could afford to buy things for their houses. Somebody made the table we had in our kitchen. Nearly all the curtains in the street were the same because the Glenfield Factory made curtain material and one of the employees managed to get enough material to go round. People used to joke that if the manager of the Glenfield Factory showed his face in the street someone had to shout a warning and the curtains would all be taken down. Maybe that wasn't a joke because I don't imagine the material had been paid for. The same system worked with paint. Anything that needed painting was given a coat of ships' paint from the local shipyard, though I doubt the owners knew anything of that either.

Our clothes were all handed down. They must have started off new with someone somewhere, but we didn't know who or where. And with around 30 of us between the two houses there were plenty of people waiting for what you were outgrowing. I remember once I hadn't quite grown into what I had to wear. My older sister, who was 18, was getting married and I needed some smart clothes. Mum borrowed a frock from a girl who was just a bit older than me. Unfortunately, as a thin twelve year old I didn't quite fill the frock, and old laddered nylons were collected from both houses and stuffed into the bits that I didn't do justice to. I can picture it still: a flowered frock nipped in at the waist and trimmed with a wide collar. I thought I was the cat's pyjamas, especially with my little artificial chest!

Other days were not quite as glamorous, such as the one when a burglar broke into our house and leant against the bed settee in which four of us were sleeping. It collapsed on us and he made a quick getaway. Being caught four in a collapsing bed settee by a burglar wasn't exactly high drama, but it did give us something to laugh about for a while. I still can't imagine what he thought he would find in a house in Ferguslie Park. All he could have stolen in our living-room were the wooden smoker's chair, the bed settee itself or the linoleum off the floor! The only thing of value was a little crystal fruit bowl that Mum loved. I think it might have belonged to her mother and I know it would have broken her heart if anything had happened to it. I only knew it was a fruit bowl because that's what I was told; I never saw any fruit in it. It was more than our lives were worth to touch it.

Saying that makes our home seem so poor, and it was. But Mum was house-proud for all that. Although there wasn't much in the house, what was there was as clean as she could make it. The bigger children in the family used to take us younger ones out to let her do the cleaning, and the floor would be covered with newspapers when we got back so that we didn't walk on it until it was completely dry. Every night Mum did the washing before she went to bed and hung it on the pulley or put it on a clothes horse to dry. Floor washing day wasn't the only time the older children were sent out with the younger ones. Sometimes we were chased just to get us out from under Mum's feet. She must have really needed that space.

Because it was a new housing scheme there were farms not too far away, and that's where we were sent for potatoes. After the 'tattie-howkers' had done their job of gathering the potatoes there were still little ones left in the ground. So when the coast was clear we took brown paper carrier bags and set off to find them. Not that the farmer knew, of course. On the way back home the string on the carrier bags cut into our hands but the thought of the meal to come kept us going. Looking back I can see that it was theft, but it was theft born out of desperation. And I don't suppose Mum would have chosen to send us to the shop with a penny to buy broken biscuits if she could have afforded to buy whole ones. They tasted just the same anyway. I especially liked going to the butcher's shop because the man who worked there sometimes gave Mum an extra sausage for me because I had such nice blue eyes, or so he said. My aunt told me later that he gave them because I was so thin. They didn't help fatten me up because any extra sausages that were going went to Dad. At Hallowe'en we earned apples and Mum made them into the most delicious apple sponge, at least it looked big until it was divided up between us. We worked hard for every one of those apples by making ourselves fancy-dress costumes from whatever we could find and going round the doors in the street singing our party pieces or saying poems. Today children think they deserve an apple and some monkey nuts when they've told a joke; we worked hard for ours.

2

'Do you want any pudding?'

I don't remember my earliest religious experience but I do remember hearing about it. Dad was brought up in a Protestant family and Mum, being Irish, was Roman Catholic. She was determined that we would be baptised but the priest wouldn't baptise us because we were from a mixed marriage, and the minister wouldn't do it either. So we were taken off to the Episcopal Church for baptism as the minister there was the only one who was prepared to conduct the ceremony. Aunt Lizzie sent her children to the chapel every week and I sometimes went along with the crowd next door. Dad didn't like it but he only put his foot down when I came home with ash on my forehead on Ash Wednesday. That was the end of my trips to the chapel.

When we were tucked up in bed at night Mum used to make us say our prayers. Every night it was the same, 'This night as I lie down to sleep I pray the Lord my soul to keep. If I should die before I wake I pray the Lord my soul to take.' I said it to please Mum; though I did believe that God was out there somewhere, I certainly didn't think he could hear me. It's strange, but while Mum told us about God, I don't remember ever learning about Jesus. The other Catholic influence on my life was a friend of Mum's. She had seventeen children and one of them, a nun, was called after my mother. Mrs Mac was a wonderful woman. People didn't need counsellors then because they shared their problems with each other. And Mrs Mac was just the kind of person the neighbours went to when something was wrong. She had a big heart, and always had time for the local children even though she already had so many of her own. Mum used her expertise in giving medicine when we refused to take it. Her friend got us from behind, held our nose with one hand and poured castor oil or syrup of figs down our throat with the other. It never failed!

As a girl of eight or nine I took a terrible headache that didn't go away and the doctor was thinking about putting me in hospital. 'Is there anything you want?' one of my aunts asked. I don't know what put it into my mind, but I told her I wanted a Bible. Maybe that made her decide that I was very ill or dying, because she went straight out and bought me a nice little one. How I loved that Bible, especially as my cousins next door were jealous because none of them had one. Having the Bible was enough for me; I didn't read it.

There was what we called a Penny Gospel Church on the edge of Ferguslie Park and very occasionally we went there. I'm not sure where it got its name, maybe from a song we sang there when they took the collection. As the pennies were put in the plate we sang:

Do you see this penny?
It belongs to me.
It's for the little children
far across the sea.
Hurry penny quickly
though you are so small;
help to tell the children
Jesus loves them all.

Before long the novelty of singing as I gave away a penny wore off. As I could think of things I'd rather do with it I stopped going.

Family life has changed a lot over the years and sometimes I smile as I think back to what it was like in the 1950s. Mum made a big pan of soup on a Saturday and it lasted into the following week. Our dinner on Saturday was a plate of soup and a jam sandwich. What we ate depended on our age, and there was a very strict pecking order. For example, when we had sausages Dad had two, the older children had one each and the younger ones halved a sausage. Occasionally for a treat we had a bag of chips between three. None of us took our eyes off the bag as it was handed round. 'One to you, one to you and one to me,' the oldest would say. And there was sometimes a battle royal when we got near the end of the bag and discovered it didn't divide evenly between the three of us. When that happened Mum or one of our older brothers usually stopped the argument by eating the last chips. We always went home from school for lunch. It was usually a sandwich, but when Mum could afford it she made potato fritters. The smell met us at the door and it fairly put a smile on our faces. Sunday night tea never varied, and there would have been a rebellion if it had. Mum made a big pan of scrambled eggs with grated cheese in it. It's not a recipe you'll find in many cookery books but it's absolutely delicious. I suppose it will be reinvented one day and become fashionable.

On rare occasions Mum invited my aunt for her tea, the aunt with the televison set. Mum could only invite her when she was flush with money because she used to buy a steak pie for four and four cream meringues. 'Now, when your auntie comes,' she would tell us, 'I'm going to ask you if you want some steak pie and I want you all to say that you don't want any, you just want chips.' That's what happened and our auntie was none the wiser. But we always fell for the trick. After watching the meringues sitting on top of the coal bunker in the kitchen all the time the grown-ups were eating their steak pie and chips, Mum would ask us if we'd like some pudding. 'Yes, please!' we all yelled, thinking of the white crumbly meringues and the thick sweet cream. 'Well you're not getting any,' Mum told us, 'because you wouldn't eat your steak pie.' See what I mean when I said my mother was clever! Although she was clever Mum was uneducated and she always had difficulty writing. She was a thrifty wee woman, and as the years passed and she occasionally had a little extra money she put it in the bank. Once she needed £20 but wasn't sure how to spell the word twenty, so she withdrew £10 on the way down the street and another £10 on the way back up.

Mothers turned their hands to everything then, hair cutting included. Every one of us had our hair cut by Mum. She had just one style, the 'start at the left ear and work round to the right ear trying to keep things even along the way'. It didn't really matter because the difference between a good haircut and a bad one is just a fortnight, and everyone else was the same. The only variation was when head lice were around and then things were a bit more brutal. Some boys used to have their heads shaved to stop them getting lice. Our shampoo was White Windsor Soap, and the only other soap in the house was Rinso for the washing done in the boiler and hard soap for what washing was rubbed shapeless on the corrugated washing board.

We only knew we were poor when we were with Dad's relatives. They had dishes that matched and they bought whole biscuits rather than broken ones. Our Wood cousins also wore shoes rather than sandshoes, though in the winter all of us wore wellington boots. Mind you, what was inside them was different. Our cousins on Dad's side wore thick woollen socks. Mum's family did what we did and wore our ordinary thin socks with the cut-off sleeves of old jerseys on top of them. And they worked very well too, though our toes still felt the cold. How I hated wearing wellington boots because they made a red line round my legs.

Another difference between the families was the sleeping arrangements. On Dad's side everyone slept at the top of the bed. I thought that was very strange as we topped and tailed, two at the top and two at the bottom of the bed settee and a whole jumble of legs in the middle. As we grew up and the older ones left home that sorted itself out and we were as posh as our cousins! The differences between the two sides of the family didn't bother me, but from when I was really quite young I knew that Mum felt it. She did her very best for us even if it meant pawning her engagement ring. Because Mum only wore it 'for good' Dad didn't realise that it was often in the pawnbrokers. When I was about seven or eight I used to take it down to the pawnbrokers on a Monday and collect it again the following Friday with money one of my older brothers or sisters had earned. Commercial travellers, we called them the tick-men, came round the doors selling things, and Mum bought what she needed from them. They came at the same time each week to collect the instalments. Once when Mum didn't have enough to pay she told me to answer the door and tell the tick-man that she wasn't in. 'When will your mother be back?' the man asked. I didn't know the answer to that question, so I yelled back into the house, 'Maw! When will you be back?' That fairly blew her cover!

There was plenty of laughter in our home. Despite the hard life she led, Mum was great fun, and most of the time Dad was too. Coming from a big family with no money to pay for entertainments meant that we often got together for family gatherings. When that happened in our house there could be more than 40 of us squeezed in. Children weren't allowed to join in the adult conversations but we used to perch on the coal bunker and watch what was going on. Our ears were pricked trying to hear what was being said, but there was such a din we missed most of it. Dominoes and cards were great favourites when the family gathered. On Saturday nights, whether or not there were visitors, there was a job to be done. The younger children got the week's newspapers and cut them into interesting shapes before tearing a hole in the corner of them and shoving them on to a nail in the WC. That was our toilet paper for the week. My granny's posh toilet roll was a source of wonder to me!

When time came for me to go to school I wasn't a happy bunny. Because there were so many comings and goings between my brothers, sisters and cousins I didn't discover until I went to school that I was actually very shy with strangers. As a result my first year at school was misery. The only happy memory I have of it was the Queen's coronation when we were each given a metal tin full of caramels. That tin became my pencil case. The coronation was a great excuse for a party and Ferguslie Park certainly partied. Women took chairs out into the street and the men sat on doorsteps. Everybody sang their hearts out. The Queen should have been there to hear them.

Eventually I settled down at school but I was never really happy there. The idea of concentrating on lessons didn't enter my head. In fairness, I think I had trouble seeing the blackboard. When it was eventually discovered that I had a lazy eye I was given a pair of National Health spectacles with a patch on one of the lenses. They did nothing for my self-esteem, and I never wore them apart from at school. Very early on I discovered that I could raise a laugh in the classroom, but while my class enjoyed that the teachers did not.

Although I came from a stable home, and my brothers and sisters seemed normal enough, I can see that even in primary school I had hang-ups. I always felt different, almost as though I didn't belong in the family. In fact, deep inside I felt I didn't belong anywhere. That didn't stop me having friends and one of them was well enough off that she often had money to go to the sweetie shop. I was right there beside her. Nannie Scott made trays of sweet sticky candy balls and they lay at the front of the counter. They kept us sucking happily for ages, but getting them was a bit of an adventure. While my friend went to the counter to pay for her sweets I leant on the tray of candy balls then couldn't get outside quickly enough to see how many had stuck to my woolly sleeve.

The only subject I enjoyed at school was Religious Education because the teacher told us the life stories of some famous missionaries. My favourite was Mary Slessor, probably because she started off as a mill girl like Mum. For some reason that I still can't explain, when I heard about the work missionaries did I knew that's what I wanted to do. I suppose it might have been the thought of the wee black babies. If I had known what a real missionary's job was like I would never have believed that one day I would actually do it!

When I was about nine years old I started dodging school. I left home as though I was going but headed for the park instead. And about the same age I took up smoking, not cigarettes but bits of cane pulled out of Mum's cane shopping basket. A wee crowd of us gathered in a cellar to smoke our canes and to make up nicknames and songs about each other. I can still remember mine. 'May Wood is not good. Chop her up for firewood. When she's dead break her head and make her into gingerbread.' Our other topic of conversation in the cellar was what we would do when we grew up. I knew my dreams. I wanted to have plenty of money and to travel the world wearing nice clothes. I dreamed of never being hungry, of there always being bread when I needed it. All our dreams were much the same.

Money was always a problem in Ferguslie Park, and part of the problem was that wives didn't know how much their husbands earned. The men were paid in cash on a Friday and most of them headed for the public house before they thought of going home. When they eventually staggered home they gave their wives 'the housekeeping' and kept the rest for themselves. Many women, and my mother was one of them, waited until their husbands were in a drunken sleep then took more money out of their pockets. The following morning the men assumed that they'd drunk it. Without that little extra some would have been hard pressed to feed and clothe their children. Mum had another trick she played on Dad. Often on a Friday he arrived back with a half drunk bottle of whisky that he put in the space on the side of his smoker's chair. When he was very soundly asleep Mum poured most of the whisky out and replaced it with water. By then he was too far gone to know the difference.

Mum hated Fridays and so did I. Dad wasn't always a nice drunk. If he'd had too much liquor he became very aggressive both with her and with us. As Dad was Benny Lynch's sparring partner we didn't hang around when things got ugly. There was many a time when we hid up the close when he came in and stayed hidden until he'd fallen asleep. It must have been the same in about half the houses in the street. The sad thing was that the new houses in Ferguslie Park were really nice. If the men who were in work had brought their pay packets home and spent the money on their families and houses the scheme might have had a chance of being a success. But that wasn't the culture. Poor children stayed poor. The houses had little or nothing done to them and before long the area lost its new look and began to resemble a battlefield. Fences were pulled down, rubbish left out in the back greens and children like myself who dodged school ran wild.

By the time I went to secondary school the rot had well and truly set in. I saw myself as a dunce and only one person tried to tell me otherwise. My art teacher told me I was really gifted. I remember him saying how nice the colours were in a painting I did of a caravan site. I didn't believe him. School made me feel stupid and I believed that I was. But I did have my uses at school. I always stuck up for the underdog. Unfortunately that meant that if a fight broke out I was right there in the middle of it helping the loser. Mum used to say that I was the one in the family who brought dead ducks home. Sometimes I even took in old men for her to make them a cup of tea.

When I was about twelve years old Mum found a job in a canteen. Every morning she got up early, laid the fire, prepared the dinner, then set off for work. For the first time there was a little spare cash, and what did she decide to spend some of it on? Elocution lessons for me! Anyone who has ever heard me speaking knows what a waste of her money and my time that was. My cousin (on Dad's side and better off) went to elocution and Mum decided that if she could go then so could I. What Dad thought of it isn't recorded but my brothers teased me like mad. Every week I trailed away to a very up-market part of Paisley where I learned poems, did breathing exercises and put my mouth into the weirdest shapes. At the end of term the elocution teacher arranged a function in the Town Hall and all her pupils had to take part in it. A big crowd of the family turned up to see the two cousins do their thing. But they only saw one. I took stage fright and couldn't say a word. That was the end of the elocution and much good it did me.

Mum wanted better things for me and she did what she could. But she didn't do what I most wanted and needed. I would have done anything to get her to cuddle me and tell me she loved me, but that wasn't in her nature. Dad was affectionate, apart from some weekends, and he would take me on his knee and cuddle me. Once, after I was married, I asked Mum why she couldn't show us that she loved us. Poor Mum, she looked wounded when I said that. 'But I do,' she said. 'I brought home half a pound of butter when I could afford it.' It wasn't easy as a young teenager to see the occasional butter on the table as love, though I know it was. I suppose that feeling unloved just sums up my relationship with Mum at that time, even though in my heart of hearts I knew that wasn't true.

3

Dredging the Depths

When I was fourteen years old I got my first new coat and beret and I was delighted with myself. The coat was green with velvet buttons. Unfortunately a long stem with a pompom came out of the beret, and as sputniks were in the news at the time I found myself with a new nickname. As being popular with my friends was more important to me than pleasing Mum the sputnik was pulled off. A pair of shoes might have gone along with the coat and beret but I blew them for a swim. I wanted to go swimming with my friends even though Mum told me there was no money. But I knew there was money in the house because she always had a little pile of shillings beside the gas meter, enough to keep us in gas for the week. When I looked to see how many were there I found two. One of them went straight into my pocket and I headed off to meet my friends. The pool cost 4d and I put the 8p change back beside the other shilling. Mum was not happy. She marched me to the Co-operative Store and pointed to a pair of shoes in the window. 'I was saving up to buy these for you,' she told me, 'but we're going right in to cancel them. And you'll stay in the house for a week as a punishment.'

I rarely made Mum happy in my teenage years. She had longed to go to school when she was a girl, and here was me coming up to school-leaving age and with very little to show for it. She was unhappy about what she knew I got up to and she would have been even more so if she'd known the trouble I got myself into out of her sight. There were gangs in Paisley at the time, there still are, and I used to run with a gang. It was made up of secondary school age children, both boys and girls. There were terrific fist-fights, boys against boys and girls against girls, and I was always in the thick of them. 'I'm going to hang out down the street with the girls', I'd tell her before leaving, knowing full well that there would be trouble and that I'd get a buzz from it.

Dad didn't see the worst side of me; Mum got it every time. She used to say that she'd brought the wrong baby home from the hospital. It may seem a strange thing to say but that's what it felt like for both of us. I had never really fitted into the family.

I was like a cuckoo in a robin's nest. All I wanted to do was leave home, to be free. But first I had to get work and earn some money, and I found a job as a stock control clerkess. It was a good job, but I lost it. Then I went to another office then another, never staying long anywhere. Eventually I took a job in a café and got to know another girl who worked there. 'Do you want to get a half bottle of wine between us?' she asked, one night. I was still fifteen at the time. I agreed. We bought the wine and went up a close to drink it. My friend took a gulp and handed it to me. Two mouthfuls later I couldn't believe what was happening to me. A warm feeling in my mouth changed to a burning sensation right from my throat to my stomach and I knew without a shadow of a doubt that I'd found what I'd been looking for for years. One half bottle of wine between two and I was an alcoholic. That might seem an exaggeration, but it's not. It's a stark fact and I knew it. I don't mean that I knew I was an alcoholic, but I knew that drink was what I needed to make me the person I wanted to be. I was hooked. My insecurity dissolved when that wine reached my stomach. The following week when my friend and I bought a half bottle we drank it between us, then I bought another half bottle to drink by myself.

Drink was only the beginning. Before long I was taking tablets bought from people who had been prescribed them. I took Valium, sleeping pills, anything I could get my hands on. These habits are not cheap and I began stealing to pay for my drink and drugs – all this before I was sixteen years old. At first I thought nobody knew what I was doing, but Mum certainly did. And she realised I had a real problem when one night I was brought home drunk and disorderly by the police. I didn't drink in public then, but up closes and in the town's toilets. Not long afterwards Mum and Dad were going away for two weeks and because she didn't trust me in the house Mum arranged for me to stay with my aunt. I had different ideas. The night before they left I stole Dad's key out of his pocket and as soon as they left I let myself in with my drinking friends. Before long Mum's spotless house was a tip as we partied day and night. When I didn't turn up at my aunt's she came to see what was going on … and there was plenty going on. She ordered us out of the house. I'm sorry to say that I was awful to my aunt and refused to leave the house. When my parents came home I did a runner and was away for two weeks. Mum had no idea where I was and she must have been worried sick. Then one night I went for a walk down a street not far away from home with a boy I knew. I looked a sight. Underneath my headscarf my hair was in rollers and I was the worse for drink as usual. I didn't hear a car drawing up beside us, and the first I knew was when my brother's hand landed on my shoulder and I was pulled into his car. He had me home in minutes. Mum's welcome was to shut me in my upstairs bedroom to dry out and come to my senses. I had other ideas. I opened the window and jumped two storeys to the ground and was off, not even hurt.

The next months were a mess. Sometimes I was at home, but all I did there was fight with everyone. Then I'd storm out, or go out and get so drunk I didn't know where home was. My family tried to talk sense into me. They tried to argue sense into me and to fight sense into me, but I spat it all back in their faces. Once after a huge blow-up with them I drank a whole bottle of wine and took a handful of pills with it. I don't know what happened after that as I was in a coma for a week. One of my sisters stayed with me as she thought I was going to die. At first I was in a general hospital but eventually was transferred to a psychiatric unit and it became my home for the next eleven months.

During that time I was in such a bad way I was given Electro Convulsive Therapy (ECT). That was a scary experience. The horrible thing about it was that when I came round after it I couldn't even remember who I was, and each time I had it I felt I lost another bit of me. I know ECT helps some people but it certainly wasn't for me. By the end of that time I was so institutionalised that I couldn't cope with life at all, so much so that I fought against being discharged. Hospital was easy. I was doped up and sat around like a zombie. I didn't have to make decisions. Nobody hassled me. I could have stayed there for the rest of my life. My family knew better, and one of my brothers argued to have my drugs reduced to allow me to become a person again.

My life became a cycle of drinking, overdosing, having my stomach pumped and being in hospital. I overdosed so often that having my stomach pumped was no big deal; I could have done it myself. I don't think I really wanted to kill myself although it felt like that at the time. I've only God to thank that I didn't succeed. Once when I was in having my stomach pumped another girl who had attempted suicide was being treated at the same time. She had slit her throat. The girl died. Still I didn't learn my lesson. Not only was I a danger to myself, but to other people too. Once when I offered a woman a chocolate she didn't just refuse it, she slapped me on the face. She was probably as drunk as I was. I grabbed a bottle to defend myself and before I knew where I was I found myself back in the psychiatric ward. Desperate for freedom (and probably for drink) I broke a window and ran. But I was caught and put in a jacket with long sleeves that were tied behind my back. I was in a straight jacket! Then I was locked in a padded cell for my own safety. On that occasion I found myself with some really wild people, even worse than me. Dad stormed up to the hospital and told them that I wasn't mad; it was the drink that was doing it. I don't know whether it had anything to do with Dad being Benny Lynch's sparring partner or not, but I was moved to another ward.

It was about that time that I started self-harming, as if drinking and using drugs was not doing me enough damage. I slashed myself many times, and once cut right up both arms one after the other. Having the first one stitched was so horrible I wouldn't let them do the other one. I still have the ragged line to remind me of it. I know that people like me were the worst possible patients, and I know that Accident and Emergency staff must have felt their hearts sink when we arrived in their departments, but what they didn't understand was what their attitude did to the likes of me. I drank and slashed my arms because I hated myself and all I stood for, so when some of them treated me like the scum of the earth they were just confirming what I felt about myself. Even though they helped by pumping my stomach or stitching me up, their approach to me made me want to go right back outside and do the same again. I'm not for a minute blaming the hospital staff for what I became; that was my fault. But I would maybe have been helped a bit earlier if they had treated me differently. And I know people who are as I used to be, who won't go to a hospital now because of the very same thing.

One night, when I was sixteen years old, I was with a pal. We had a television by then and Dad was at home watching a boxing match with some of his friends. One of my older brothers arrived at my pal's house. 'You need to come home,' he told me. 'Mum wants you.' 'Why are you wearing a black tie?' I asked. He turned away. 'I put it on because I was in such a hurry to come,' he said. Our curtains were closed when we arrived, even though it was bright daylight. 'Why are the curtains shut?' I asked. My brother didn't answer. A neighbour was scrubbing the stairs and we had to pass her. 'If I'd known about your father I wouldn't have started scrubbing the stairs,' she apologised. And the truth stabbed me. Dad was dead! My dad was dead! I kicked her bucket of water down the stairs and bolted for our door. Grandpa Wood was there, crying his heart out. 'It should have been me,' he cried. 'It should have been me, not him.' I went berserk. I'd never experienced death before and it knocked me sideways. Eventually Mum had to send for her sister to sit with me because I tried to jump out the second floor window. Maybe I just wanted to die to be with my dad. For the next few days I was doped out of my mind. I went to the crematorium, and went back to it late that night. Mum was worried sick about me and the whole family went out to look for me. One of them went back to the crematorium and found me there. I was in such a bad way I ended up in the psychiatric hospital yet again. I was utterly shocked that Dad could have been fit and well one minute then have a thrombosis and be dead the next. It went round and round my mind like something haunting me. The day Dad died was the worst day of my young life, and there had been some horrible ones before it.

After that my life didn't so much go from bad to worse, as from worse to worst. I stole to pay for drink and drugs, sometimes on my own and sometimes with other people. Once I went with another girl into a shop and we stole a frozen chicken that we could resell. It was a cold day and she had on a furry hat. We were both under the influence. She grabbed the frozen chicken, shoved it in her hat and put her hat back on her head. A mixture of the drink and the cold from the frozen chicken got the better of her and she fainted at my feet. I didn't know whether to haul her out of the shop, put the chicken back, or walk away and pretend I'd nothing to do with her. I could 'earn' a lot shoplifting. Some days I'd take two outfits from different shops, one to wear that night and the other to sell on. That sounds as though my appearance meant a lot to me. The truth is that by then I'd lost any self-respect I had.

The police knew me well and often picked me up and took me home, or to the cells for the night. Sometimes if I wasn't out of my mind with drink they would take me quite a distance from Ferguslie Park so that I would sober up on the long walk home. I ran away often, sometimes intentionally but mostly I went when I was blind drunk and didn't know what I was doing. In the morning I would wake up in London or Folkestone or even Ireland and not have the first clue how I got there. Guilt piled up on me as the months went on. I hated myself when I was sober, and hated myself even worse after I'd been on another bender. Sometimes I looked at myself in a mirror and knew that there was nothing, absolutely nothing, that I liked about the person I was looking at.

Some drunks are quite entertaining, some whinge and some are violent. Sadly I was often a violent drunk. Many a time the police picked me up fighting and took me home to my mother. 'Here's your daughter … drunk and fighting again', they would say, as they hauled me in the door. That poor wee woman took me in and washed the dirt off me before half carrying me to my bed. Mum bailed me out of more trouble than she ever deserved to go through in her lifetime. And the horrible thing was that when I dried out I knew that, and it added to the burden of guilt I was living with and sent me back for another drink. When I was sober I used to look at my brothers and sisters and ask myself why I was as I was. I'd had the same upbringing as they had, better really as Dad and Mum had a little more money when I was growing up, yet I was the one to go wrong. My poor mother must have been asking herself the same thing; I know my brothers and sisters were.

By the time I was seventeen the family had had enough, and who can blame them? I was beaten up and somehow managed to get to my aunt's house. She took me home and told Mum that she'd done all she could for me and that I should be sent to America where I'd have the chance of a new beginning and the family could have some peace and quiet. A cousin was in Jersey at the time and I suggested that Mum give me the money to get to the Channel Isles and that I'd make a new life for myself there. She agreed. I took Mum's money and left Paisley, sober for a change. I met up with my cousin in Jersey and, like the prodigal son, as long as Mum's money lasted I had plenty of friends. It didn't last long. I had several jobs, one after the other, but I was drinking as hard as ever. One night my cousin and I stole a car and went for a joyride. Unfortunately we crashed the car, though we climbed out of the wreckage unhurt. The next day I heard about the crash on the Jersey news, and that the police were looking for two people from Glasgow. I did another runner and ended up in Blackpool. When I arrived there I was drunk, penniless and destitute. Hungry and cold I slept on the streets for a couple of days before making a reverse charge call to Mum's neighbour to ask my long-suffering mother to wire some money to the Blackpool Post Office for the bus fare home. I don't even want to think what Mum's feelings were as she did it. She must have had a very heavy heart. Years later that cousin became a Christian, and he is still going on with the Lord.

Mum knew exactly when I was due home and she was ready for me. My bed was made up, the water was heated for a bath and there was a big pot of stovies waiting to welcome me home.

4

Miracle in Mayhem

After returning from Jersey I got work in a Paisley café. A man who knew me from coming into the café I used to work in kept asking me out. Eventually I did go out with him though the family wasn't pleased about it. He had been married and divorced and he had three children from that marriage. As usual I paid no attention to the advice I was given and agreed to marry him. We argued even before we were married so I really don't how why I expected things to be better afterwards. They were not. Although it was some years and two children later before he divorced me, I am not going to write about our relationship because my husband is now happily remarried. I'm really pleased about that.

I can hardly believe some of the things I was involved in during the years I was married, but they help me to remember the depths that can be reached, and I hope and pray that they keep me from ever feeling proud. A friend of mine had an old boiler and we knew some people who worked in a distillery. They stole white raw whisky, bottles and tops, and I bought colouring. Together we put the raw whisky into the boiler and coloured it to perfection then bottled it for selling or sharing with our friends. We could have killed ourselves and them too. A woman I knew in Ferguslie Park drank so much undistilled whisky that she died. We didn't supply it. When we were working on it anyone coming in the close was nearly knocked over with the smell of the stuff.

Three years into our marriage we had a beautiful little baby daughter. We called her Tracey. But although I promised that wee girl the world my life continued in a downward spiral. Sometimes I left her for days and went off on my own. Once I even ended up in Ireland where a social worker found accommodation for me overnight in a Christian hostel and put me on the boat back the following day. I've no idea how I got there as I hadn't the money to pay the fare. When you are in the kind of drunken state I used to get myself into you don't know where you are and what you are doing, and you have no memory of it afterwards. Once when I was locked up in a police cell I even set fire to my clothes. Thankfully the policeman on duty came in time to put it out.

Tracey was dressed in the best of clothes from the best of shops because I looked for quality when I was shoplifting. What my little daughter lacked was not nice things but her mother. She had a great deal of loving from my mother and sister who did all they could for her, but although I loved Tracey more than I can say, I still neglected that dear wee girl. If I were to let my mind wander down the road of what I was like as a mother when she was little I could go on a massive guilt trip. But I can't let myself do that because God has forgiven me and, amazingly, so has Tracey. I thank the Lord every single day for my daughter and for the loving relationship we now have. When I see her with her children I get such a thrill, because despite all the neglect she suffered from me she is a Christian and a most wonderful mother.

When Tracey was ten years old Alan was born. Most of my pregnancy was spent in the psychiatric hospital. I remember looking at him the day he was born and thinking how lovely he was. He was just beautiful. Tracey had been a beautiful baby too. I didn't sleep the night after Alan's birth; I just wanted to keep looking at him. My mind couldn't take in that such a beautiful baby could have come from me. I was terrified to lift him up in case I contaminated him. And before the night was through I promised Alan that he'd have a very different kind of childhood from Tracey. I'd love to say that was the end of my drinking. It wasn't. For the next two years I was as bad as ever. Mum and my sister Anne were wonderful. When they knew I was drinking they would come and take Tracey and Alan away and keep them until I was sober again. Sometimes they were with Mum more often than they were with me. Mum and Anne were Gods gift to the children. I certainly wasn't. And they were Gods gift to me, for despite all I'd done to them over twenty years they never gave up on me.

One morning I woke up out of a drunken sleep. Tracey was at school and Alan was still toddling around in the same clothes he'd worn the day before. Even his nappy hadn't been changed. He was two years old. When I looked at him it was as though my eyes opened to let me see what I was doing to my children. I got up, changed and fed Alan, then went to see the only person I knew who would let me into her home. She had been an alcoholic but was by then a Christian. My friend took me in and gave me a cup of tea. 'What are you doing tonight?' I asked her. 'I'm going to a meeting,' she replied. 'Can I come with you?' My friend looked at me. 'No,' she said. 'You can't. Look at you. You're filthy. Your clothes are a mess and covered with cigarette burns. And you smell.' 'I'm coming!' I told her. 'No you are not!' The more she said I wasn't going, the more determined I was to go with her. Saying no to me always made me rebellious.

That night I followed my friend to Glasgow and went into the building behind her. It was a church and she was going to a Stauros meeting. I was embarrassed, not for me but for the other people there. They all looked so respectable and I was an absolute mess. They read the Bible and a man prayed, 'Lord, I pray for that wee woman you've brought here tonight. We can all see that she's filthy by looking at the outside of her, but you know how much more filthy her heart is. Touch her and clean her.' He prayed for me and all I could do was cry because I thought I was so worthless that I wasn't worth a prayer. There was a cup of tea after the meeting and I was more relaxed then. Coming from a big family meant I was first in the line for tea. As I was drinking my tea a man asked for a word with me. I went with him into a wee room. 'Do you want to be saved?' he asked, after he'd spoken to me for a minute or two. I was puzzled. 'Saved from what?' He was so patient. 'Do you believe in God?' he enquired. 'Yes,' I replied. 'I can honestly say I believe in God. But God doesn't want anything to do with the likes of me.' 'God didn't send his son Jesus to die for good folk. He sent him to die for sinners. Are you a sinner?' the man asked. 'I'm the worst there ever was', I said, then broke down and cried my heart out. Before I left that room I asked Jesus to come into my life. There were no flashing lights; nothing spectacular happened. I didn't know what was meant to happen anyway. But I knew that things were different. It was 22nd September 1981.

Charlie Mallone

I remember May coming in the door to the Stauros meeting. She looked a right forlorn wee soul, nervous and shaking.

She sat down and was quiet all through the meeting. After the meeting was over one of the other men there told me that he thought the new woman would like a word with me. So we took her into another room and spoke to her about her need. May didn't have any idea what we were talking about, but she said that she wanted whatever it was that we had. I told her that five years ago I'd been just like her. She was so surprised. It hadn't occurred to her that we had all been alcoholics. 'I'd love to be like you all,' May said. I told her that God could change her heart and make her the same as us. She wasn't convinced. 'I've done too many bad things in my life,' she said. I explained to her that Jesus died on the cross for bad people, that he died for sinners. My friend and I were like two beggars telling another beggar where to find bread.

That night my life changed completely and people saw a difference right away. All my life I'd felt as if there was a piece of me missing, and that night I discovered that what was missing was Jesus. I didn't have a Bible, but during the night God gave me a verse from the Bible. 'I will restore to you the years the locusts have eaten' (Joel 2:25). I hadn't a clue what it meant. But God soon led me to someone who could tell me. A pastor at Stauros showed me that the verse was in the Bible. He even showed me the place. When I explained that I didn't have a Bible he gave me one. The pastor explained that God had given me that verse to show me that he would give me back all the years that I'd wasted with drink and drugs and self-harming. I was thrilled.

The day after I was converted I cleaned the house from top to bottom. It had been filthy. When I was tidying a cupboard I found half a bottle of whisky. I poured it all down the sink and the only alcohol that I've drunk since then is sips of Communion wine. Right from the day I was converted God made me a missionary. Nobody at the Stauros meeting told me that missionaries were special people who did years at college and had to learn a foreign language to do their work. And because I didn't know that I became a missionary immediately I was converted. Everywhere I looked I could see poor people just the same as I had been and I had to tell them about Jesus. The thought of them going to hell horrified me and I had to do something about it. The day after I was converted, as soon as my house was clean, I was on the street telling people what Jesus had done for me.

It must have been interesting for the people who knew me. My neighbours were amazed at the total change. They watched for me coming up the street drunk, and at night they listened for the police car stopping at the door and a couple of officers taking me home drunk and incapable. Instead of cursing and swearing at them when I saw them I stopped and talked to them about Jesus. Some asked me what had changed me and I wasn't slow to tell them! A number of my neighbours were thrilled, and I suppose they were also relieved because it couldn't have been very nice living near me. Others raised their eyebrows when I told them about my conversion and I could just see what they were thinking. They thought that drink and drugs had at last taken their toll and that I'd lost my senses completely. The truth was that I was talking sense for the very first time. Even several taxi drivers, who knew me well from picking me off the pavement outside pubs and taking me home, stopped and asked what had happened.

I continued to go to Stauros meetings and was helped a lot there. Stauros is an organisation for alcoholics. The people there believe that every need can be met at the cross of Christ, and that even alcoholics can find healing there. Stauros is the Greek word for cross. It was there that I met Pastor Arthur Williams who explained what the verse meant. The Bible he gave me was well read. I could hardly stop reading it! Just days after I was converted Arthur was speaking at a meeting. He quoted the verse that says 'We are living stones' but he couldn't remember the reference. I was able to tell him what it was! 'She's only been a Christian for days and she knows her Bible chapter and verse,' someone commented. I loved reading the Bible. It was like food to me. One evening we were sitting in a circle discussing what we'd like to do with our lives. The last time I'd done that was when I was a girl and went with my friends into a cellar to smoke cane and discuss our dreams. But that night was different. 'I feel God's wanting me to be a pastor,' one man said. And he did train as a pastor. 'I want to be a teacher,' said another. And that's what he went on to be. When my turn came I didn't know what to say, then I heard myself saying, 'I'd like to have millions and millions of Jesus' love so that wherever I go it will spill out on the people I meet who are unwanted, not needed and unloved.'

There was one man I desperately wanted to talk to, the psychiatrist who had looked after me for years. I phoned the hospital and asked to speak to him. He probably thought he was going to get a drunken tirade. 'Dr S,' I said, 'I've got the answer to a lot of your patients' problems.' By then he was no doubt sure I was drunk but he waited patiently to hear what I had to say. 'When I was in your hospital I was doped to the eyeballs and sat around for weeks like a zombie,' I told him. 'And in that state you can forget your past and all your shame and guilt. But when the drugs wear off the shame and guilt are still there. Drugs don't take them away.' I was so excited as I went on with my good news. 'Dr S, Jesus Christ has taken away all my guilt and shame. It's as though he took it from me and put it in a river beside a sign that says "No fishing". I can't fish my past up now and neither can anyone else.' When Dr S realised that I was stone cold sober I don't think he could believe what he was hearing. I've met him and some of the nurses from that hospital since then. 'You're a miracle,' one of them told me. I agreed, and explained that I was a miracle of God's grace.

Probably nobody was happier at what had happened than Mum. I explained that I'd become a Christian and that I had to make amends for all the hurts I'd caused her. 'You don't need to make amends at all,' she told me. 'The amends are made because I can go to bed and sleep at nights without listening for the police coming up the stairs to tell me that you are in prison, or the hospital phoning to say you're having your stomach pumped.' To show how much she trusted the new me Mum gave me a key to the house. I'd not had a key since I stole Dad's one when I was fourteen years old. Some years later, when Mum was dying, she said to my auntie, 'I can go away and be with my Maker now for I know that May is all right.' Those were her last words. And she did go to be with her Maker because Mum also became a Christian. That was one of the most wonderful ways that God restored the years that the locusts had eaten. He gave me back to Mum and he gave Mum back to me for us to love and appreciate each other.

God showed me that there were places where I had to make amends. When I was drinking I once stole money from a collection box in a church and I went back to repay it. The old minister had gone away and a new one was there. I gave him £5 and explained that it was for repayment and amends. 'I can't accept this,' he told me kindly. When I insisted and explained that God had shown me that was what I had to do, he took the money. Over the years I've seen just the same thing happen with new Christians. The Lord has shown them too that they have to make reparation for what they have stolen or damaged.

Another thing the Lord did was show me what was right and wrong. I'd been living in a drunk world for so many years that I'd lost the sense of right and wrong. For example, I worked each morning as a linen maid in a local hospital and I was quite happy to take 'freebies' – cleaning things and the like. We didn't feel we were stealing when we did that; we thought we deserved it because we were so badly paid. Whole streets in Ferguslie Park were cleaned with 'freebies'. When I was converted God showed me right away that taking things from the hospital was theft. So the next time I was offered them, I explained that I'd become a Christian and didn't want to take any more. It was hard to do that as the woman thought she was doing me a favour. Not only that, the people I worked with immediately became suspicious of me and thought I would tell the bosses what they were doing. I wouldn't have done that. Being a linen maid meant I could talk to the patients about Jesus as I went round the wards with the linen.

I worked in the hospital because I had to. There was no money to spare and what I earned was needed to help pay the bills. When I was converted God showed me that there was a bill I had to pay that I'd avoided for years. Like many others in Ferguslie Park I had fixed my electricity meter which meant that we didn't pay for our electricity. It was quite a thought to make the meter work properly and to pay for what we used, but God supplied the money I needed to do that out of the money I wasn't spending on alcohol.

I had one bad slip after I was converted and it's not fair to tell my story without mentioning it. My Bible was at the bottom of the magazine rack under all the papers and I was very far from God, though I wasn't drinking. One day three pastors came to the house, I can't remember why there were three of them, but I'm ashamed to say that I swore at them and told them not to come back. They left. When I woke up the next morning I saw my Bible under the pile of rubbish, and God spoke to me. He showed me that my life was exactly like what I was seeing in front of me, that I'd put a whole pile of rubbish on top of Jesus. I'm not one for opening my Bible at random and reading what's in front of me, but I did that day. The verse my eye fell on was, 'Greater love has no-one than this, that one lay down his life for his friends. You are my friends if you do what I command' (John 15:13-14). My heart was broken. 'Lord,' I said, 'you're calling me a friend after all of that.' There was a knock at the door; it was one of the pastors. 'Come in, Jimmy', I said, and went on to tell him about God's word to me. Jimmy looked at me before speaking. 'May, I want to tell you something. I didn't sleep a wink. I've been praying all night for you. And God showed me that I'm to give you this tape.' The tape was called *You are my friends.*

5

Reflections of a Local Doctor

I was born in Paisley and have lived and worked here most of my life. When I was young the town was quite a self-contained place, certainly not an adjunct to Glasgow. We had our own bus service with links to the city. Two thread mills in the town provided major employment. Engineering, food processing, textile dying and finishing, the production of glue, as well as shipbuilding were all labour intensive. Factory horns were heard all over the town, and people knew them apart and could tell the time by them. In the post Second World War years the industrial pattern gradually changed. Several factories closed, and in 1983 the mills shut down. Linwood, famous for the Hillman Imp car, had been built to help ease the unemployment situation.

The Ferguslie Park area of Paisley was developed in the late 1920s and early 1930s to give people good housing that was to greatly enhance the quality of their lives. The streets were well laid out and the buildings of good quality. Most were tenements two or three storeys high, though there were a few with four storeys. The town was very forward looking in its social policies. The first tenants came from the old central tenemented area of the town, from housing first built round about the mills to house the workers. The mills then employed about 13,000 people. It was like the end of a football match when the mill horns sounded and the shifts changed. Special tram services operated to fit in with the shift patterns.

This housing development should have been a success but it failed to reach its potential and ambitions. Folklore has it that some people kept coal in their baths, and doors could on occasion provide emergency firewood. Alcohol became a problem, and poverty was real. But in the midst of it all there were some fantastic people, families with a real ambition to better themselves. I remember one lad, whose family roots were in the area, who went to a famous university and graduated with an honours degree. Part of the area was served by the medical practice in which I worked. Although there was a problem with violence when I was a young doctor I never felt threatened. Doctors then had a kind of status that afforded them some safety. Here I met real people with many problems, both social and medical.

Some years after the Second World War considerable unemployment became an increasing reality. Drink was a persistent problem. Within a few decades Ferguslie Park changed from a hopeful new housing scheme to an area marked by despair. In 1947 May was born, though I didn't meet her until she was an adult. In the 1950s, when she was a child, more housing was built and she moved from one of the older houses to a new block. The family lived on the first and second floors. She was probably delivered by one of the splendid midwives who served the area. They weren't only midwives, they were counsellors and friends as well. People who needed advice often asked the midwives even if there was no baby in the household. Having said that, there was usually a baby as big families were very common.

May's generation of children in Ferguslie Park was often poorly nourished, and not through maternal neglect. A high proportion of income was spent by men in the public house before going home on a Friday night if they were in work, and if they were not, their wives were fighting a losing battle to keep their children well fed and decently clothed. At that time to be poor meant to be really poor. I have memories of seeing bairns drinking milk out of HP sauce bottles with teats attached. Babies' bottles were a real luxury. When visiting patients in the area there were children everywhere, even at 10pm. Of course, childhood diseases thrived in those conditions. Interestingly, there was no public house in the scheme, or in the adjacent housing schemes. People went into the town centre to drink. It was when the public houses there closed that trouble started.

Over the years Ferguslie Park became an isolated place. It was not the most popular residential address in the town, and if you had an alternative you certainly didn't accept a local authority house in that area. Ferguslie Park, locally known as Feegie, was tough. Eventually people had less chance of getting a job if they gave a Ferguslie Park address. Having said all that, many of those who did live there were survivors. The area produced winners and losers, and the winners were strong, strong people. They had to be. That was May's environment as she grew up.

I first met May in my capacity as a local doctor, and calls to her home were not anticipated with any degree of enthusiasm. I recall one late night visit when I arrived to find a real fracas in full swing. May could be quite good at hurtling things around, at doctors too on occasions. When

I arrived to make this visit I found the entire tenement brightly lit. The noise was such that nobody around was able to sleep. It was obvious that May had been drinking heavily and she might also have taken tranquillisers. She was bawling and shouting, cursing and swearing. Her house was in utter chaos. It was a very difficult situation altogether, particularly as she had slashed herself, both her wrists and abdomen. As May was pregnant at the time she required immediate hospital admission. Following a time in the acute hospital, she was transferred to the psychiatric hospital, not for the first time. By then she had a long history of alcohol and drug abuse as well as self-harming. May was a woman going nowhere, a poor soul lost in the world.

Eventually I lost touch with May and never expected to meet her again. One night two members of Stauros came to speak at a meeting in my church. I didn't recognise either of them. As the informal meeting progressed, one of the speakers, a woman, pointed at me and said, 'Doctor, you will be able to confirm all that I'm saying.' When she saw my incomprehension, she said, 'I'm May Nicholson. Don't you remember coming to help me?' To use a very modern expression, I was gobsmacked! I suddenly realised who the speaker was and my mind immediately turned to my last meetings with May in the late 1970s. She was a totally different person. When I knew her previously she was a deeply depressed alcohol addict with no hope and her life going nowhere. She seemed in utter chaos. Now May was completely and utterly different. The transformation in May's life was as dramatic and complete – yes, miraculous – and in many ways similar to the change in Legion's life when he came face to face with Jesus some 2,000 years ago. This encounter is detailed in the Bible, in Mark 5:1-20. It's an amazing story; you should take time to read it.

After Legion was restored to his right mind, Jesus sent him back to his own people to tell them what the Lord had done for him and the Lord gave May the same commission. He sent her right back to Ferguslie Park to tell the people who knew her as a no-hoper that there was hope in Jesus. And just as Legion's friends were amazed to see the change in him, I know that May's friends must have been equally amazed. Many people she meets know that she is not talking academically, that she has been where they are. The truth is that May would not be able to do the work she is doing now if she had not been through the things she went through.

May, my wife and I are now members of the same congregation and it gives us a thrill to see her and to hear about the work she is doing. When we began our relationship I was a doctor who dreaded a call-out to May's address, and she was a patient in dire straits and not always welcoming. Now we are sisters and brother in Christ and we praise God for the miracle of grace he has performed in May's life.

6

Home at Last!

As a teenager I occasionally went to the youth club at the church in Ferguslie Park just to torment those who went there. That was the extent of my church attendance. After I became a Christian I went to the church because I knew that's what I should do. The first time I went to a Sunday afternoon service the minister, Chris Park, was speaking about persecution. There were about half a dozen people there and I felt really sorry for the minister because when he stood up in front of the others and spoke to them he got no feedback at all. I didn't realise that was what services were like! In the couple of days before that Sunday I had been reading a book about a pastor in Poland who was persecuted for preaching. His church was taken away from him and he had to work as a rat catcher to feed his family. But that didn't stop him talking about Jesus. As he wasn't able to preach in church he went round the villages near his home town telling the people he met about Jesus. At the end of the service Chris asked if anyone had anything to share. I told the little group of people there about the book I was reading just to remind them that God is always glorified, in a tiny congregation as much as in a huge one, and in a Polish village street as much as in that persecuted pastor's church.

As soon as I began attending church I felt completely at home. That was amazing, because my life had been so rootless there was nowhere that gave me that kind of feeling, not even my own home. I sat right at the front – typical me! – and drank in what the minister said. Then, and in the years that followed, I learned more from Chris's ministry than I can say. I was utterly ignorant about Christianity and he patiently taught me from the Bible. I will never be able to thank him enough for that. Instead of longing for drink I found myself longing to take people to church so that they could hear what I was hearing. From then on I knocked on doors inviting people to come to the service with me. It was such a natural thing to do. I was at home in the church and it was like inviting people into my own home. And I was so worried at the thought of people going to hell I was desperate to get them where they would hear about the Lord and what he could do for them. Before long the minister asked me to do little things in the service. Chris really nurtured me in the Christian faith. Now I try to do with others what he did with me.

At the same time I became very involved in the work of Stauros. Because I was converted at a Stauros meeting, and was released from my addictions there, I wanted to help however I could. Soon I was giving my testimony at meetings. The first time I was asked to tell how I became a Christian I was petrified! I got up to speak and halfway through I dried up. Not a word would come. Then I said that none of my family would believe that May Nicholson was lost for words! The people at the meeting laughed and that gave me a minute to think. Occasionally after I'd spoken I'd find myself just amazed at what God had done. A few months earlier I'd been a no-hoper drowning my sorrows in drink and drugs, using every way I could think of to escape from myself, now I was standing up in front of groups of people telling them that Jesus had forgiven me for all that, and that he'd released me from my addictions. God was very good to me because he took me off drink and drugs without any of the terrible withdrawals that many people go through. I don't know why he did that, but I had to remember it wasn't the same for everyone when I was speaking to those who were trying to come off. Another thing that amazed me was that God used my testimony to help people from all sorts of backgrounds, poor folk like me and wealthy professional people too, people who wouldn't have looked at the ground I stood on before I was converted. Over those months I saw wonderful things happening in some folk's lives.

God spoke to me after I'd been a Christian for about six or seven months. I don't mean that I heard a voice speaking in my ears, but I heard him in my heart just as clearly as I heard people actually speaking to me. He asked me why I didn't do the work I was doing through the church. I approached the minister and asked if this was a possibility. 'You'd have to give up your job to join the team,' Ian Maxwell, the associate minister, pointed out. I thought about the money I earned as a linen maid and hesitated. Ian realised that we really did need that money and offered to help find support for me. Before long financial support came from Ireland and England as well as different parts of Scotland. There was no response from Wales!

Not long afterwards I was out visiting with someone else from the church. We always went in twos. That night I learned a lesson that has stayed with me. Although it was the right time for me to reach out to people, I still had a lot to learn. We visited a woman and found she was a spiritualist. During our talk together she said things that I knew I wanted to forget. Later things kept coming back into my mind that she had said, horrible things that really disturbed me. Over and over again I repeated the name of Jesus, asking him to take them away and eventually the dark thoughts went out of my mind. I realised then that there were situations in which I needed to call in someone who had much more experience. Although I was full of enthusiasm I was short on experience.

After working with Chris and Ian for a short time it was suggested that I should become involved in working with alcoholics and drugs addicts through the church rather than through Stauros. I prayed about it then discussed it with Arthur Williams, who ran Stauros in Glasgow. 'Praise the Lord!' he said. 'That's what Stauros is all about, helping the church to do its own work.' He fully understood the needs of Ferguslie Park and the openings I would have there if I worked through the local church. Ian and I then started a little group, though it didn't stay little for long. We decided to call it Kairos, which means 'the right time'.

Through Kairos I had contact with both alcohol and drug addicts and drug dealers too. One dealer took us into his house to show us a big rug he had hanging on his wall. It was a picture of the Lord's Supper. The man told us that his daughter was going into hospital and that he wanted us to pray for her. We did. Nobody would think of a drug dealer having a huge picture of the Lord's Supper on his wall, but maybe that man was like me when I knew there was something missing from my life.

It took me years to discover that the missing piece was the Lord Jesus. Perhaps he suspected that was true of him too, or he might just have been superstitious.

One woman we visited was a widow who had turned to drink when her husband died. Every time I went to see her she gave me drink to pour down the sink and assured me that she'd not drink ever again. But as soon as I left she used to phone and ask a taxi driver to go to an off licence and buy her some alcohol. Eventually she was converted, and other members of her family too through what she told them and because of the difference they saw in her life. As we were looking for a new venue for Kairos she invited us to have our meetings in her home. Sometimes 50 of us squeezed in! We had great times of praising God and praying over our worries. God gave Ian Maxwell, our associate minister, exactly the gift we needed. He could just sit and share the gospel simply. He didn't preach or rant and rave, he just said what was in his heart and it often went right to the hearts of some of those who were there. There were nights that felt like revival time. Ian and I had a very easy-going relationship and that helped too. Although Ian's wife Ellen wasn't involved in that side of the work, she was a wonderful support and I learned so much from her. People like Ian and Ellen were God's gifts to me as I began to grow up as a Christian. I was so clueless that I needed their mentoring.

My work has always been about people; I'm a people person. The story of my work is just made up of different people's experiences, and that's really all I can share in this book. I've already mentioned some of the people who were converted and who grew to be fine Christians, but that didn't always happen. Sometimes things started well and ended up tragically. That was true of one man especially, a man who came from a notorious background. He attended our Kairos meetings and was very much a part of the group. We were thrilled when he seemed to come to faith and it really looked as though God had changed him. But he started welcoming his old friends into his home, friends who were still taking and dealing in drugs. At first he didn't take them himself, then he took a little, then more. One night he wrote a letter saying that he couldn't live in this world any longer. Having signed the note, he took a drug overdose and died. I knew Jesus' story about seeds falling on rocky ground and sprouting up and looking hopeful though they had no roots, but it still hurt so much. The whole group was really wounded by his suicide. Mum used to say that if you fly with the crows you get shot down with them.

One night there was a rally arranged in the church and we decided to go round all the doors inviting people to come. We walked up and down the streets with some of the young people playing their guitars and singing. Not everyone was pleased to see us and we were even stoned by some people! We were not the first Christians to whom that has happened. The stones didn't stop us; we just kept going. So many people came to the rally that the church was full to overflowing and people were converted who are still going on in the Christian faith. The stoning was worth it! Numbers are not what it's all about, but they do show that something's happening. On my first visit to a service in the church there were only about half a dozen people there, months later about 60 were attending Sunday worship. Many of the newcomers came from outside the church, people with problems who came in. It's not always easy for a church when that happens but the people in St Ninian's were brilliant. God was doing good things.

If there were any rich people in Ferguslie Park I never met them, but I met plenty of folk who were struggling to make ends meet. The church there was very practical. For example, when one young mother's flat flooded and her carpet was ruined everyone chipped in and bought her a new one. The Bible says that the believers shared what they had. That's what we did too. And we helped in other very practical ways. One home I visited was filthy because the woman who lived there had never been taught how to clean. We made arrangements for her to spend time with another family who ran their house well and the difference was amazing. That woman was converted and she now keeps her house spotless. She does it as if she is doing it for the Lord. I had to remember that myself in the work I was doing. Yes, I was working for the good of the people of Ferguslie Park, but the bottom line was that I was doing it for Jesus. If you think like that then only the best is good enough.

Knocking on doors is no problem for me because I can talk 'the hind legs off a donkey'. But sometimes it was helpful to have something to give to those who answered their doors. That's why we ordered large quantities of back copies of Challenge newspaper. We didn't just push them through letter boxes, rather we visited in twos, knocking on doors and chatting to the people before handing Challenge over. One day a woman answered her door to my companion and me. She said she was just going into hospital for an operation and if it wasn't successful she would go blind. We talked to her and prayed for her. Next time we took Challenge to her door she was smiling. Her surgery had been a success and she believed that God had heard and answered our prayers. As a result of Challenge our visits and the prayers of the people of St Ninian's, all of that woman's children began to attend Sunday School – and there was about a dozen of them.

As I went round the streets of Ferguslie Park I was very conscious of young people hanging around with nowhere to go and nothing to do. When that's the case trouble often follows; and it did. That's why the church had to be guarded, and why cars were always in danger of being vandalised.

Young people today have different expectations to those we had. We were poor and our only hope of being better was by our own hard graft. Some of those we met in the streets knew they were poor but they felt hard done by and angry at society. They thought that the world owed them better than they had, that they had rights that were not being met. Rights hadn't been invented when I was young, or at least I'd not heard that I had any. The ministry team and other volunteers tried to get alongside these young folk. God blessed the work and in their ones and twos they began to be converted. Those who became Christians befriended others and so the work went on. Youth With A Mission (YWAM) eventually took on the work and it continued for several years.

Moira Park, my minister's wife, wanted to start a women's group and she and I worked together on it. We met in a young woman's house and eventually about twenty came along. The meetings always started with prayer because we wanted to feel God's presence with us. Over the winter we did study courses like '*God Change Me*', and in the summer the meeting had a family feel about it. For example, the women once took their children to sing to the residents in an old people's home. Several women came to faith at those meetings. Although I was helping to organise them I learned such a lot at them, especially from Moira.

My mother was one of the best home-makers I've known but I was so rebellious as a young person that I didn't allow myself to learn from her. It was in Moira's home that I was taught things I could have learned from Mum. When I first started visiting her I was a very new Christian and still doing things like shouting at Tracey and Alan if they annoyed me. I watched Moira with her children and saw that she was very different. She was gentle with them, and when they were naughty she talked to them rather than screamed at them. I could hardly believe her patience, especially as she had five children! A verse in the Bible tells us to imitate the good in one another, and I learned to mother Tracey and Alan from imitating the good in Moira. I'll always be grateful to her – and they should be too!

Money was tight but God never saw us hungry. On one occasion I had a call from a woman in another part of Glasgow. She had a drink problem and wanted to speak to me. I had £2 in my purse, and I knew that if I went to see her the bus fare would use up the money I had for the next day's dinner. When I told Alan about her, he said, 'It's OK, Mum. God will provide.' He'd heard me saying that so often. I did go and the visit was really worthwhile. On my way back a man stopped me and said, 'Are you wanting to go to a wee meeting in Paisley?' I went. At the end of the meeting I was given an envelope that had been put in the offering plate. It had my name written on it. I opened the envelope and found £10 in it. 'God hasn't just given us potatoes,' I told Alan. 'He's given us strawberry tarts as well!' That wasn't the only time Alan taught me a lesson. One night we were walking home from a visit together. It was dark but the moon was shining. Then a dark cloud went over the front of the moon. 'Sure that's just like us, Mum,' said Alan. 'We have the light of Jesus then the devil comes just like that big black cloud and tries to block out Jesus' light.' Out of the mouths of babes!

Around the same time someone from the Brethren Assembly up the road from the church phoned and said that the people there would like to give me a gift. They had heard about the work I was doing and, as they knew how big Ferguslie Park was because they also worked there, they decided to give me an estate car to use in the work! They taxed it, did everything else to get it ready for the road and gave me £200 for driving lessons! I joked that it would take £20,000 to get me through my test. And it would have done too. But God had better things for me than driving lessons. He had a driver ... but that's another story.

One night Ian and I got a call to make a home visit. We knocked at the door and a young man answered. 'Is your Mum in?' I asked. She wasn't. 'I'd take a cup of tea from anybody', said I, and the young man took the hint and invited us in. His name was Cammy. Before we left three hours later we had heard his sad story. Cammy, who took both drink and drugs, had been in prison for attempted murder. He was not in a good way. Not long before our visit he had spoken to a spiritualist who told him to seek God. Having had a really bad experience with a spiritualist in the past, I just sat and listened to what Cammy had to say. Ian and I arranged to see him again, and that was the beginning of something very wonderful. God used those visits because a few weeks later Cammy became my driver ... then he became a Christian!

Like me, Cammy was a missionary as soon as he was converted. In the first house I took him to visit we found a man in a drunken stupor. 'What will we do here?' Cammy asked. I suggested that we cleaned the place up and gave him a surprise when he came round. So Cammy's first job as a missionary was to gather vomit into polythene bags. That's just the kind of thing Jesus would have done in that situation. God showed me that I should train Cammy and I did that by taking him with me on my visits. After a while working together we decided that we should go to college. Me go to college! We enrolled for an English class in the local college. The English teacher used to write 'Wow!' at the side of our essays until we told her they weren't from our imaginations but from real life as we knew it. At the end of the course we both passed the exam! Later the woman who taught the course asked me to go in and give talks to the college's social work students.

That wasn't the only studying I did. As we found ourselves counselling people with problems Moira Park and I decided we should do some training. So we attended a counselling course. I think we knew it would be good for us personally as well as helping us in the work we were doing. Today I still use the counselling skills I learned then. But I don't take on more than I can cope with and refer people to other counsellors when they need more than I'm able to give. Before I was converted I would have laughed myself silly if anyone had suggested that I'd have gone to college to train as a Christian counsellor!

Back to the car. I never did pass my driving test but Cammy was there to drive for me. He did a few hours work as a taxi driver each day to earn enough to live on and gave the rest of his time to mission work in Ferguslie Park. The car lasted till the end of my time there, though it changed quite a bit over the years. By the end of its life it had four different coloured doors, all bought from the local scrap merchant. It certainly made the car recognisable. We called the car Joseph because of his coat of many colours! That car was very well used. Apart from taking us wherever we needed to go, it was used to do hospital and prison visiting, removals (often with its boot open and a wardrobe or cooker peeking out), and to take families who really needed a break on holiday. I lost count of the times Cammy and others took people down to places like Stevenston where they could pitch a tent free of charge and enjoy a break. It was also perfect for filling up with elderly people to take them for a cup of tea at Loch Lomond. That car could have been called 'Blessings'!

7

Cammy's Story

Rev Cameron MacKenzie

When I was a young man my home life was very difficult. Alcohol played a big part in my parents' marriage breaking up. I lived at home with Mum and my brother. He had mental health problems so severe that he once set the house on fire. My brother's situation became even worse after a motorcycle accident in which he lost a leg. Every single month seemed to bring new disasters and none of the old ones ever went away. Our family was an accident waiting to happen. After the fire Mum spoke to a lady in the corner shop who asked if a visit from someone in the church would help. Mum agreed to that. At least it couldn't do any harm.

I was then working as a taxi driver, and about the same time I was having long discussions with a customer who was a spiritualist. She really freaked me out because she told me all sorts of things about my life, things that she couldn't possibly have known without some sort of special insight. It was a supernatural experience, but a very scary one. The woman told me that a spirit was saying that I had to seek God, that he was the only one who could save me. I think she wanted me to seek God through spiritualism, but I hadn't gone as far as doing that when there was a knock at the door one night when I was in on my own.

I opened the door to find two people there, a man and a woman. 'Is your mum in?' the woman asked me. I explained that Mum was out. Then she said that she'd take a cup of tea from anyone. As you don't get a louder hint than that, and because I was feeling lonely, I invited them both in. They were Ian Maxwell and May. When I discovered they were visitors from the church I told them all about my discussions with the customer. They were quiet while I talked. Knowing May as I do now I realise that it was quite something to keep her quiet for so long! 'If you want to seek God,' Ian said, when I'd finished my story, 'you should seek him through Jesus. It's only through Jesus that we can find God.' That left me thinking, because the spiritualist hadn't said anything about Jesus.

During their visit, which lasted three hours, Ian and May heard my life story including the fact that I had a drink and drug problem. 'Would you like to come to a Kairos meeting?' May asked, then she went on to tell me what Kairos was. Before they left I agreed to go, more because I liked Ian and May than for any other reason. But when I went to the meeting I wondered what on earth I was doing there. I saw myself as something of a Jack the Lad, and here I was in a group of people who couldn't have been more different. They were obviously alcoholics and drug addicts. When they spoke it turned out that several of them had broken marriages. Not only that, some weren't even very clean. I knew I had a drink problem but

I certainly didn't identify with many of the people at that Kairos meeting.

It's strange, but although I didn't fit in I did keep going. Probably that had a lot to do with May. She doesn't let people go easily! I even took my brother along but after a few weeks he said it was rubbish and stopped going. The meeting was held in somebody's living room in a council house in Ferguslie Park. Between 40 and 50 people were there; as many as could crammed themselves into the living room and the others stood in the hall where they could hear what was going on. Sometimes there was a real sense of God's presence at those meetings. This really blew me; I'd never come across anything like it before. Although Ian was there, and brilliant at explaining things, May was the driving force. I think she was driven by her deep, deep faith and trust in Jesus and her love of people, all people, not only those with problems. This was in April 1987.

Before long I was working with May, and a most unconventional person I found her to be! But that's not a criticism. She has quite extraordinary gifts, and perhaps the main one is that she sees potential in people even when other folk only see problems. May sees the fire in them and is able to fan it up and direct it to where it will be useful, even in people who aren't Christians. That's what she did with me. Within two or three months of meeting me May had me driving her around in the car she'd been given for her work. That suited me perfectly as I was a taxi driver. Having said that, I worked the taxi just to earn money for drink and drugs. May was aware of that and I was never under the influence when I was driving her car. She wouldn't have stood for that!

When she knew me a little bit better May suggested I went with her to a Stauros meeting and I agreed to go. That night a man preached about Jesus. When he'd finished speaking May turned to me and said, 'What about you, Cammy? Are you not going to be saved?' But I had a surprise for her. 'I was saved last night at home in my bedroom,' I replied. May's face was radiant. There is nothing in the world that gives her such a thrill as when someone trusts in Jesus. Since then I've discovered that for myself. By the time we were back in Paisley that night I think May had a missionary's life planned out for me! In practice that meant driving the taxi three days a week and driving for May and working alongside her the other two. Before long we had a really close working relationship. May teaches by example. She doesn't say, 'Watch how I do this or listen to what I say here'; she does it and says it and you learn from her. I saw that what she did worked and copied her.

May was exciting to be with because she was where things were happening. I believe that is partly because God has made her a people magnet. She likes a challenge and she likes to touch people. The folk who knew May in her drinking days used to ask how she could be so alive and such fun without drink. The truth is that she was never really alive all the years she was drinking; she only came to real life when she was converted. God took the ruins of her old life and refined them, so freeing her to be what he meant her to be in the first place. What you see now in May is something of the divine image. You should be able to say that of every Christian. I think the area in which I saw that best, both in May's life and in Ian's, was the way they related to my brother who had problems. They didn't write him off even when he wrote them off. Seeing them in his company made a deep impression on me because they treated him with dignity.

Dignity was sometimes in short supply in Ferguslie Park. One night May and I were out late visiting. On our way home we passed an elderly man pushing a walking frame with a carrier bag hanging from the handle. We drew up beside him and asked if he needed help. The poor man had been discharged from hospital that day and the carrier bag was full of his hospital things. I helped him into the car. We had to open the windows pretty quickly as at some point in the day he hadn't managed to reach the toilet on time. He told us his son's address and we took him there, but the young man wouldn't take his father in. In the absence of an alternative we took the man to May's house then phoned a Christian centre we knew to see if they could accommodate him as circumstances meant that May couldn't keep him overnight. Just when things were becoming problematic the centre phoned back and offered him a bed. By then we had cleaned him up and he was enjoying a cup of tea.

Four months after I met May my taxi badge was taken from me for a drugs offence committed before I was converted. I'd been a drug addict for seven years. By then I was working with her two days a week. God opened the door for me to become effectively the fourth member of the ministry team in Ferguslie Park and I found myself working alongside Chris Park, Ian Maxwell and May. I had no professional training and I lived by faith, receiving no pay for the work I did. For the following two years we were involved with broken families, people with drink and drug addictions and mental health problems. At its most basic level we were just loving people and trying to draw them to Jesus and into the church, and we could only do that because it was the kind of church that was prepared to be supportive.

Nearly everyone in the area was quite poor, both financially and socially. Few of us had had any opportunities or had taken any we had. May opened our eyes to a world outside ourselves. She used to organise trips to Ireland, and they were quite something. Fifteen of us would crush into a transit van with no windows in the back to drive down to Stranraer for the ferry to Larne. In those days we all smoked which meant that we were nearly kippered by the time we arrived. When the back door was opened to let us out a cloud of smoke must have escaped before we did! As May had contacts in Northern Ireland, in places much the same as Ferguslie Park, we were made very welcome. When we were there we did street evangelism and beach missions too. Nothing daunted May. If she saw an Orange Lodge building or a UDA club she knocked on the door, explained that we were a Christian group from Ferguslie Park in Paisley and expected to be invited in. We were, and we told them what Jesus had done in our lives.

May is the most efficient people magnet I've ever met. She can meet someone at a bus stop and start a conversation that will mark the beginning of a friendship that will last for years. Her desire is to get to know people and to introduce them to Jesus. I remember on one occasion May was in hospital for an operation. During the night she got out of bed to go to the toilet and when she came back an elderly lady was in her bed. What an opportunity to make friends! May did just that and for years afterwards we visited that lady in her home, and her daughter and granddaughter too. Youth With A Mission came to work in our part of Paisley and I became involved with the work they were doing, even going to Romania with them. May caught the vision and took a group of Fegs (people from Ferguslie Park, and not an offensive expression) to Romania. Even the language barrier didn't stop her communicating with the people we met! She took several groups there and they did a good work. But I'll leave May to tell that part of her story.

I wasn't many months old as a Christian when the Lord showed me that he wanted me to work for him full time. What kind of work that would be I had absolutely no idea, but as I knew that it would likely involve some kind of training I decided to study for O-Level English and Religious Studies. May said she was going to do English with me; maybe she wanted to encourage me. But perhaps that wasn't her motivation. There is a vulnerable side to May and studying for O-Level English and passing it gave her a real sense of achievement. It did that for me too. Our English teacher thought we were very imaginative because of what we wrote in our essays, and she gave us very high marks. Eventually we confessed that all we wrote about was real life as we had known it.

As I attended that class, for the first time in my life I got something out of education. The teacher was a real lady; I think she was Canadian. I'd never met anyone like her before. She inspired us to think and showed us what we could do. In that respect she was like May with her gift of showing people abilities they don't know they have. We found out a great deal about ourselves in the two years we studied English together. And the day the results arrived and we both discovered that we'd passed was one I'll never forget!

About this time there was word of May perhaps moving away from Paisley to work elsewhere, and there were big changes in my life too as God showed me that he wanted me to apply for the ministry. May was almost as delighted when she heard that as she was the night I was converted. I can still hear her voice, 'Aw Cammy, that's pure dead brilliant!' (Although Irene has written her story in English that's not exactly how May speaks!) She was so thrilled that God had taken me, a total waster, and turned me into someone he could use, and that he had allowed her to be part of it. She was behind me all the way.

What I've said about May shows that she's a very driven person, and that doesn't always make her easy to work with. In her own way she's quite feisty; she'll fight for her lambs. From time to time there's a weakness in that kind of drivenness but by far the majority of the time her drivenness is God-glorifying. Part of the problem of working with May and those like her is that they are successful in what they do and that can make the people they work with feel vulnerable. So being part of a team of which she was a member was quite extraordinary and wonderful … and occasionally we tore our hair out!

After studying English along with May I did a one-year mature students' access course along with several others heading for degrees in divinity, then I went on to Glasgow University where I studied for four years full time before graduating with a Bachelor of Divinity degree. Strangely, although I'd gained nothing whatever from my time at school, I took to further education like a duck to water. At first I didn't know whether God was calling me to the ministry in Scotland or to go overseas to work for him, but that became clear about halfway through my course. At the end of my first year I went to Brazil for the summer with Youth With A Mission to work with street kids in the town of Belo-horizonte and there I met Dilma who, in 1993, became my wife. Two other holidays were spent along with May taking groups to Romania. By then she had moved to Dundee and I did what I could to support her there. I think that the role God gave me at that time was to be a big brother to Alan. That was a real privilege. May was always there for me and I tried to be there for Alan.

I became minister of Garvald and Morham linked with Haddington West Church in Lothian in 1997. And I just love it! May spoke at my ordination which was very special for both of us. That same year our son Pedro was born, and two years later the Lord gave us another son, Lucas. Looking back over my life, and remembering the situation I was in when Ian and May knocked at the door, I can hardly take in all that God has done. May is one of his best gifts to me, though it's really hard to define our relationship. At one level we are friends, but she has also mothered me and been a sister to me. We are colleagues in God's work too. Perhaps I should just enjoy May rather than trying to work out the mechanics of our relationship. And I can do that because whatever else she is, May is great fun.

I'd like to share some of the things I've learned from May over the years that have stood me in good stead both in my ministry and in my own Christian life. She showed me that everyone matters to God, and that the most important thing you can do for people is to help them see that they are special in his eyes. May also taught me that the main things to set our minds and hearts on are winning people for Christ and helping bandage their wounds. On a daily basis she displayed to me good and clear that it's not enough to have a message, you have to live the message too. In my times with May I learned that we must let people participate in the work and not just leave them as spectators. When they are doing the work of the Lord they grow in the Lord. Finally, I think May's life expressed for me how utterly we are dependent on Jesus alone for all we need – but that we still need to get our sleeves rolled up! Thanks May!

8

Good News for Ferguslie Park

Rev Ian Maxwell

In 1982 my wife and I returned from working overseas and joined Rev Chris Park as Associate Minister in Paisley's Ferguslie Park. Andy Kennedy was also part of the team; he was a Youth and Community Worker. Although Ferguslie Park was just a council housing scheme it was as big as some small towns. When I was there the population was between 7,000 and 8,000 people, and all of that on what had been a 1930s green-field site. The houses ranged from substantial 1930s – 40s cottage style or three-storey houses to 1960s Lego blocks. None were more than four-storey buildings. There was one long three-storey building nicknamed the 'Queen Mary Building', because when the lights were on it looked like a ship at sea. Ferguslie Park was spared the high-rise flats that proved such a social disaster elsewhere in the Central Belt. Many of the families were respectable

*working people, but a few tenants were put there because
the council had nowhere else for them to go. Sadly one or
two bad tenants in a staircase could make everyone else's
life misery, sending them off to the council offices to ask for
a transfer. In the 1980s unemployment was a real problem,
especially youth unemployment which sometimes affected
90% of that age group. Rather than being able to name
the few teenagers who were out of work I could name the
few who had jobs. The closure of the Linwood car factory in
May 1981, which had provided employment for thousands
of people, was a real body blow to the area.*

*For all its problems Ferguslie Park had a real community
spirit. We were there just before the wholesale breakdown of
marriages, and traditional family relationships were still
the norm. I can remember several places where married
daughters lived in flats in the same closes as their mothers.
People put their children outside to play assuming they
would be safe. It wasn't at all unusual to see quite small
children playing in the light of a lamppost after 10pm. They
seemed to be able to keep going even after I was beginning
to wilt! Unlike some council housing estates Ferguslie Park
has a centre. There is a roundabout in the middle of the
area and the estate's main roads radiate out from it. As St
Ninian's Church of Scotland is right next to the roundabout,
everyone going anywhere has to pass it.*

*That was the background against which May suddenly
burst into our lives. I remember being in Chris Park's
living-room doing some typing – those were the days before
we all had computers – when the doorbell rang. Chris
answered it and brought a woman into the room. 'This is
May', he said, and introduced me to her. In the conversation
that followed I discovered that May had been brought up
in the area, that she was an alcoholic and that it was only a
few weeks since she had been converted through attending a*

Stauros meeting. She was looking for a church to attend and had started coming to St Ninian's. My first impression of May was that she was very outgoing and friendly, and by the time she left that day I was caught up in the enthusiasm of her newly found faith. She was just bursting with new life. There are few things more infectious than spending time with a young Christian.

Nothing then could have shown us (or warned us!) quite what an impact she was about to have on us and on the life and work of St Ninian's. One of the great blessings of the months and years that followed was the deep Christian friendship that grew up between Chris and Moira Park, May and later Cammy, and my wife Ellen and myself. May's openness and warmth helped us all to relax; but it was more than that. Our friendship was a friendship in Jesus. Her love of Jesus is at her very heart and it spills out into everything she says and does. Because Christians have one heavenly Father they are brothers and sisters of each other. That's a fact, but we are not always aware of the reality of it. In May's company the reality was almost tangible. The Holy Spirit seemed to hold the little group of us close to each other and close to him. The first months of knowing May was almost like a process of discovery: we discovered a friendship, and we discovered a deep fellowship in Christ. Later, we discovered that we were brought together at that time and in that place because God had some very rich blessings in store for us all.

Chris's job as minister was very arduous. He could have been on the go 24 hours a day; there was so much work for him to do. The parish was huge, the problems were enormous, even just keeping the routine things going would have been a full-time job. We agreed that I should work alongside May part of my time, in particular when reaching out to people with alcohol or drug problems. Consequently, my relationship with her continued to deepen. Although we are from very different backgrounds the things you might think would separate us didn't do that at all. We instinctively trusted each other absolutely, and in a strange way we found ourselves working as a unit. For example, May is a real visionary, but when we were discussing and planning our work she didn't announce that she had a vision of what should be done and expect me to fall in line with it; she was able to include me in seeing the vision in the first place. I suppose that comments on the working and personal relationship we had at that time more than anything else I could say.

In other circumstances May arriving in a congregation might have felt threatening. I don't think that was the case in St Ninian's at all. The church had quite a small core. An outsider wouldn't have known the people or the local situation, but she wasn't an outsider and she knew the area and the people as well as the members did. Of course, some of them knew her from her past, and were so amazed by the change in her life that her enthusiasm swept them along and they went willingly. In a way she actually wore her qualifications for working in Ferguslie Park on her own body. The slash marks on her arms from where she tried to take her life on many occasions were like badges that proved she fully understood the problems, heartaches and challenges of life. You might remember that Paul once said, 'Let no-one cause me trouble, for I bear on my body the marks of Jesus' (Galatians 6:17). Well, when people sometimes asked May what the marks on her arms were, she would say, 'These are the marks of my old life, but the life I have now is a new one in Jesus'._

May was a huge help in all kinds of ways. For example, at one of our ministry team meetings – it was around 1987 – May suggested to Chris and me that we could start *a Bible study. We looked at our jam-packed diaries with sinking hearts. But at that time May was beginning to explore areas of service, and we asked her if she and I could work together on the project. She knew a man, an alcoholic, in the area and thought that we could have the Bible study in his home. We discussed it and decided to go ahead. What started off as a Bible study with a handful of people (one or two alcoholics among them) more or less grew into a Stauros meeting. In her all-embracing way May used to welcome those who came to the meeting with, 'I don't care who you are, or what problems you have, because you can find help here. In a minute or two Ian is going to say a wee word to you.' With that she opened the door for me to speak about Jesus.*

Through May three things happened at that time. The first was that doors were opened for me into lives and situations to which I would otherwise have had no access. Some of the people I met through May would never have darkened the door of the church. And although I might have met them on the street, we would have walked past each other. There would have been absolutely no point of contact between us. Secondly, a role developed for me simply speaking from the Gospels rather than preaching sermons. I didn't set out to be deliberately spontaneous but much of what I said was in response to the questions people asked at the Bible study. But apart from that, the pressure of work was such that sometimes by Friday night I was so utterly exhausted that delving through commentaries to help with my sermon preparation was more than I was able for. There were times when I felt like Peter. He and the other disciples were out at sea one night when a terrible storm blew up. In the midst of their fear they saw Jesus walking on the water towards them. Peter asked if he could walk on the water and Jesus called him to do that. At first things went well, then Peter's faith faltered and he started to sink. Jesus reached out and gripped his hand and all was well. At the beginning of some weekends, after an exhausting and sometimes traumatic week, I had to reach out in faith to Jesus for a word to say.

The third thing that happened was that both May and I grew in understanding of what Jesus meant when he said, 'Where two or three come together in my name, there am I with them' (Matthew 18:20). We began to realise that even if, on some wet winter evenings in Ferguslie (and there were plenty of them!), there was only May and myself and a couple of others, that was enough – and it always would be enough – for Jesus was always present. It isn't just sentiment; it is fact. Whether there were 54 of us together or 'only' four, it didn't matter. Jesus was there with us, always ready to bless.

Six or seven months after beginning the house Bible study circumstances necessitated a change of venue. We moved to the home of a woman who had not long before lost her husband. Like many of May's friends (she would never have called them 'contacts') she had a drink problem. We wondered if the move would make a difference as it was in another part of the estate and a bit off the beaten track. At the same time we changed the content of the meeting. Instead of going right into a meditative kind of Bible study we started with a time of praise. People seemed to appreciate being together and the cup of tea after the study went down well too. The meeting put down roots there and began to grow. About then we gave it the name Kairos, which means 'the chosen time'.

Opportunities arose that saw May beginning to deploy her evangelistic gifts more fully. I used to watch her relating to people and wish I could do it as naturally. She would speak to a woman on the street who would be the cousin of a man two streets away who needed help. Then someone would come up to her and say, 'There's been a great change in Bill.' 'It's from the Lord', May would say, as we walked on, only to be stopped by someone else who wanted to speak to her about a problem. She seemed to attract people like a magnet, and not only those with problems. I've known individuals who were always helping people because it satisfied a need in them; they needed to be needed. There is nothing of that in May whatsoever. She loves people just because they are people, and she lives to introduce them to Jesus, the person she loves most of all.

Having a regular meeting gave May a base from which she could work and a place to which she could invite people. She visited many alcoholics (always in company, as it was our policy to work in twos) and she would say to them, 'I've been where you are, and I can tell you what Jesus has done for me and what he can do for you.' If any interest was shown people were invited to Kairos. On one occasion, when we had a visit from some representatives of Stauros, 65 people were crowded into that woman's house. There were so many that people had to sit on the stairs and upstairs too! One night we noticed a group standing outside, obviously watching and listening to what was going on. We were singing at the time. I thought that there might be trouble brewing, but they had gathered outside to listen to the praises we were singing while they dealt in drugs. They had come to laugh at us, but instead they stayed to listen.

Eventually we also began using a small room in St Ninian's for meetings. Between 30 and 50 attended, many of them with addiction problems. And it was in the course of that work that May spoke to the woman who ran the corner shop ... who asked Cammy's mother if she would like a visit from someone from the church. And the rest, as they say, is history. After Cammy's conversion, if he and May heard of *an urgent need anywhere in Paisley they were there, a kind of flying squad carrying the good news of the gospel of Jesus Christ. Over the years 1988 and 1989 the group meeting in the church hall became a conduit through which many people came to church. Because so many of them smoked they gathered for a cigarette on the church steps before the service and everyone else had to fight their way through a cloud of smoke to get in. Not quite your traditional welcome! The Spirit of God moved very strongly among these people. Chris facilitated the work through the church and supported us in every way he could, and May was the outreach worker. I have always been grateful that I was able to be part of it all.*

One of the things Christians are guilty of is hanging on to organisations after their work is done. Towards the beginning of 1990 it became clear that the work of Kairos had been done and that God had blessed it mightily. But changes were afoot. Chris and I would soon be moving away from Ferguslie Park, and it seemed that May was to leave the area too. We arranged one last Kairos evening and had a wonderful time of praise. Yes, there was such a lot to thank God for, and as we thought of all that he had done in individual lives as well as in the life of the church, we could only give thanks. And still today, when I think of those years I am grateful to God.

Rev Chris Park

When I think of May and the story of her journey with God, there is one Gospel passage that often springs to mind. It's the story of the 'sinful woman' who washed and anointed Jesus feet (Luke 7: 36). When criticised by the owner of the house, one of the 'righteous people', for letting a person with such a dodgy reputation do this to him, Jesus commented that those who have been forgiven little, love little. By contrast, those who have been forgiven much (as this woman was) love much. I hasten to add that I don't mean by this that I'm implying May was a much greater sinner than the rest of us! But when we first met her, she certainly had a very low sense of self-worth and felt profound shame over her past life, overshadowed as it was by her drinking and all that went with it.

When May first heard the gospel through the work of Stauros, she was overwhelmed by the realisation that God loved her, despite all that she had been and done. May could profoundly identify with the way Jesus accepted that woman in the story, without condemning her, and that filled her with a sense of amazement and gratitude that went to the very core of her being. Out of that encounter with the amazing grace of God, May began to discover that she could become 'a new creation' in Christ: that the 'old has gone and the new has come' (2 Corinthians 5:17). In the months and years that followed, like the proverbial butterfly emerging from the chrysalis we saw a new May, though not without her share of struggles and pain.

This unconditional acceptance of her by God became the fertile soil for her developing ministry of compassion and personal evangelism. She was able to communicate this sense of acceptance without the barely concealed disapproval or awkwardness that so many of us can feel when in the company of people whose lifestyle is worlds apart from our own. Even though this sometimes may have felt a bit like a friendly steamroller that wouldn't take no for an answer, May has the ability to break through people's fears and defences to win their trust and build a meaningful relationship with them.

This wasn't just a matter of words alone, however, even though May's ability to speak the language of the drinker and identify with his story has been a central part of her ministry. She has always been very quick to roll up her sleeves and put love into action – whether cleaning up the vomit of someone drying out at 3 o'clock in the morning, arranging for a young, impoverished family to have their first holiday for many years, or tracking down some basic items of furniture to replace what was sold to buy drink. Her sense of humour and generous hospitality also helped to disarm people who might otherwise have felt suspicious. Many she met had grown accustomed to being used and had forgotten what it was to be invited into someone's home for a meal.

This love-in-action, born out of her conviction that God loves people whatever their past life or present circumstances, has allowed many to begin to feel something they had lost long ago. Hope. Those of us who have been spared the experience of plumbing the dark depths of despair little realise what a precious and powerful thing hope is. When people saw in May the change that God's grace is able to make in someone's life, and when they realised she wasn't going to give up on them (often despite many a disappointment and rejection) they began to dare to believe that there was hope for them as well: that their lives could be different, that they could begin again too. And many did, and continue to do so.

May was an enormous encouragement to me personally in my ministry. Her hunger and enthusiasm for God's Word and her love for Jesus were a delight to see, and her desire to bring others to church so that they could also find faith was an inspiration to us all. Her prayerful support and friendship were often a source of strength to me in difficult times. Through her work with Ian and the Kairos group, a significant number of people started coming to our church in Ferguslie Park. That was thrilling, but not without its problems too. It's not an easy thing for a small congregation to find itself full of newcomers, some of whom were still obviously enjoying a bucketful! And sometimes the vitality and enthusiasm of those who had just come to faith could be quite threatening to those who had held the fort for many years in very difficult circumstances. In our enthusiasm to see people in Ferguslie find fullness of life in Christ we were not always as wise and sensitive to one another as we might have been – we were all on a steep learning curve! During such times of change and intense experience our personal insecurities and pride, not to mention jealousy, can come to the surface making us defensive and critical, instead of listening to and learning from one another.

But God in his grace held us together and before long mutual trust and respect grew. I remember how one of our long-standing members discovered around this time to her dismay that one of her family had a serious drink problem. Her initial reaction was one of shame as well as incomprehension; but partly through talking with May she came to see her situation in a new light and learnt to cope with it well. She went on to be very supportive and appreciative of May's work and helped others in the church to see it very positively.

Someone from another part of Paisley, who felt really bad about his drink problem and was desperately looking for help, spoke to the minister of a different church in the town who had heard about May's remarkable work. He suggested that this person go along to the church in Ferguslie because he'd heard there were 'loads of drinkers and sinners there'! We had May to thank for that! If Jesus really is the Friend of sinners, and if he really did come to seek and save the lost, then I'm sure he was mighty glad to have a 'sinful woman' like May to wash and anoint the feet of his body, the church. And so was I.

9

Passport to Dundee

Ferguslie Park was my home, and I put heart and soul into the work I did through St Ninian's. It was really hard graft but the friendship and fellowship of the ministry team and the support they gave me meant it was one of the happiest times of my life. God really blessed what we did and the church grew amazingly, so much so that other people came along who could do what I'd been doing. At that point the Church of Scotland was looking for an outreach worker in Dundee and I was asked if I would consider going there. Dundee! I'd lived in Paisley all my life and Dundee sounded almost like abroad. However, when I thought and prayed about it my mind began to clear. Tracey was by then a lovely young woman and just about to be married. She would then have her own husband, her own home and her own life. Alan was eleven and in the top class of primary school. From both their points of view it wasn't a bad time for me to move. And when I looked seriously at St Ninian's I realised I had worked myself out of a job. It seemed that God might be asking me to go to Dundee after all … and I discovered I didn't even need a passport!

The base was Mid Craigie and I was to work with Mid Craigie Parish Church and the local Scottish Episcopal Church. A house would be provided for Alan and me, and I was told I didn't need to live in Mid Craigie, that I could have a council house in Linlathen, the neighbouring housing scheme and a nicer one. Whoever thought that up didn't understand either me or the work I'd been asked to do. As I knew from experience in Ferguslie Park, living in the area is really important. Mid Craigie, in the East End of Dundee, was recognised as the least desirable part of the city, both by the residents and the local authority. Shops were boarded up even though they were still open. Going into some shops felt like going into holes in the wall. Metal shutters were pulled down over other shop windows every night at closing time. They had to be or there would have been no glass by the next morning. In Mid Craigie there were many burnt-out flats boarded up and just left. And other windows were boarded over too. The scheme had the highest level of unoccupied housing in Dundee. In many ways the place looked as derelict as Ferguslie Park. Unemployment in Mid Craigie was twice the national average, and the residents had the city's lowest life expectancy. Of course, it was because the place was in such a state that the churches wanted a project worker there.

The flat we were given was on the ground floor in a typical street in Mid Craigie. It wouldn't have won any prizes for beauty or amenities, but it was home. When I looked out the window I could see my work in front of me. Fences were pulled down, there was vandalism everywhere and the children were unkempt. A stranger to the area might have thought the place was the pits, and that no self-respecting person would live there. But in a way I wasn't a stranger; it was my kind of place. I knew that behind the curtains there were grannies looking after children because their daughters were working their hearts out to feed and clothe their families, that there were men working long hours to earn enough to live on. I knew before I was told that there were parents breaking their hearts over their drug-addicted children, that there were girls in their young teens with babies. And I didn't need to wait until my first Friday night to discover that alcohol was a problem. People asked me if I thought it was fair to bring Alan to live there. But Alan had been part of the work in Ferguslie Park. He knew what it was all about and he understood why we had to live where we did. He was only eleven, but he was right behind me. If anything it was harder for Tracey who was left behind in Paisley. Part of my heart was left with her.

The churches I worked with were very supportive. They prayed for me even before the work began, and they helped me in every way they could. So as I describe the work I did you need to remember that I was doing it with help and support, not on my own. By nature I'm what Scots call a blether. I can talk to anyone, anywhere and for any length of time. To me a stranger is just a friend I've not met yet. Because of that, starting work as a project worker in a new area didn't hold any terrors for me, what did was being away from the people who could change a light bulb or replace a fuse! Having been brought up as one of the youngest of a big family there were some things I still had to learn.

A walk down to the shops in Mid Craigie for the things I needed meant people knew I had arrived. They already knew who the flat had been allocated to, and they were on the lookout for us. In that kind of area people are not slow to ask questions, and neither am I. Within a few days I knew many of the people round about, and they had already begun to share their life stories with me. I had a suspicion that after I'd talked to some folk they went down the street and told their friends that there was a wee woman up the road who would listen to their troubles. They must have done something like that because people came to the door almost as soon as the mugs were unpacked to give them cups of coffee. Nowadays Alpha Courses and other study groups have discovered that people relax and feel free to talk and to listen if they eat together. I could have told them that twenty years ago!

Before long my home became a drop-in centre for the area. Being on the ground floor helped. People would knock, pull up the sash window, pop their heads in and ask if they could come in for a blether. The counselling course I had done really came into its own then as most of the work I did was on a one-to-one basis. Many of my neighbours came to the house, but our being there must have been a culture shock for them. Suddenly they were living next to a house of refuge. When people came who were in real need they often stayed overnight. It was quite a squeeze as there were already four of us in the flat: Alan and me, a teenaged girl who was with us from a children's home, and another person who needed somewhere to stay. It was males in one room, females in another, and the extras of whichever sex in the living-room.

Not everything was done from home; I also worked in the churches that supported me. My Management Team was great and helped me organise a lunch club and midweek meeting in one of the churches. I met with them every Wednesday and without them I couldn't have done the work. Tim and Margaret Edwards prayed with me late every Wednesday night and we said we could set the clock by the fire engine sirens. At 10 o'clock exactly we would hear them racing to yet another fire in Mid Craigie. We were given a caravan that we put right in the middle of the scheme. That was wonderful! It was open from 10pm until the early hours of the morning and young people came in on their way back from a night in the pub or disco. The idea was that we would sell hot dogs and hamburgers, but as they had spent their money before they reached us very little cash ever changed hands. Ashley Cummins, the minister of the Episcopal Church, was a great help in the caravan. He had a good way with the young folk and was able to get alongside them. Adults are often shy to talk about religion, but teenagers aren't. They are really interested, and even if they laugh at you it's often just a cover-up. It was exciting news to many of them that Jesus was a real person and that he could be a real personal friend.

Much of my work was done by visiting homes, sometimes doing door-to-door visits, but most of the time following up people I had been told about or seeing those who had asked me to call. Everybody's story is different, but sometimes I felt I'd heard them before as I listened to alcoholics, drug addicts, or their husbands, wives or parents. I heard stories of abuse and violence, of poverty and despair. It would have been so easy to load myself with other people's troubles and sink under the weight of them if I hadn't had a heavenly Father to pour my heart out to and a Management

Team, ministers and friends who would listen when I needed to talk. I'm sure that there were many praying Paul's prayer: 'And the peace of God, which transcends all understanding, will guard your hearts and your minds in Christ Jesus' (Philippians 4:7). God answered that prayer and my heart and mind were kept despite the terrible things I heard and saw, and Alan's heart and mind were kept too.

There was one night when I specially needed all the support I could get. We were working in the caravan when a little boy ran out of a close screaming. I followed him back to the house to see if I could help. When I opened the door a man was just about to hit his wife with a bottle. After I'd taken the bottle from him I was told what had happened. That wee boy had seen his mother being assaulted. No wonder he was screaming. I felt so angry with God for what had happened, and that was something I had to think through. Sometimes it's hard to see God's gift of free will as a blessing when people use it to commit brutal acts. I worked with that woman for a while and managed to do some practical things to help her. God spoke to me about the situation, and I believe he told me that I was there to break the chains that bound her man. Quite independently of me he became a Christian in prison and that was the beginning of his family coming to faith.

That situation was frightening for their son, but there were times in Mid Craigie when I was the one who was frightened. One night I heard motorbikes roaring outside. Alan looked out the window and told me that there were about 50 Hell's Angels racing up the main road near us. For a minute I was scared, then I remembered back to my drinking days when my whole life was filled with fear. We did have a break-in when all the windows were broken and the house smashed up. I had been in Paisley with Alan, and Cammy ran us back home ... to devastation. Hours later someone came and apologised for the break-in! He told me they had 'done the wrong house' and that it wouldn't happen again! That was thanks to the people I knew in the criminal world. I was friendly with the wives and girlfriends of some of the lads who had done the job, and there is a kind of honour among thieves. It certainly kept them from doing the same thing over again. Cammy was a regular visitor to Dundee and a real big brother to Alan, who missed his big sister. With his help we organised missions in Mid Craigie, and we got quite a name for ourselves for walking round the streets singing with our guitars and collecting young people as we went. By the time we reached the church for our rallies we looked like Pied Pipers in Hamlin rather than missionaries in Mid Craigie!

When I was a drunk I could never have gone to church because I would have been scared of contaminating the respectable people there, and many folk in Mid Craigie would have identified with that. By the time I was working in Dundee I knew that the church was full of sinners who had been saved, and some who were not yet Christians. But the folk I was working with didn't know that. Something in them made them want to go to Christians for help, but they weren't sure of their welcome. Part of my work was to be a channel between where they were and where the church was. One way of doing that was holding meetings in my home. On Thursday evenings a few people from church came to the flat and anyone else who wanted to came along too. There were children and old people, a real mix. We had some wonderful evenings of singing and talking and praying about the things that worried us. Sometimes we sang action songs, and I can remember us standing in a circle doing one particular song when I caught sight of myself in the mirror on the opposite wall. My hair was everywhere, I was red in the face and I just wondered what some Christians would think if they'd walked in! I hope they would have grinned and joined in the song.

That Thursday night meeting made a difference to a number of people. One man, who was quite shy, brought his guitar along and played for us. He was amazing because he could make up songs on the spur of the moment about whatever was happening that day, even about what was going on in the room at the time. Lonely people came and felt welcome because the whole thing was so relaxed. The atmosphere on Thursday nights was loving, and people who feel rejected and alone recognise love when they feel it. Folk sat around on chairs and on the floor; they were everywhere. Our times of prayer were very special, partly because people prayed in the same kind of voices as they spoke to each other. I know Christians who have one voice for God and one for other people, but my friends in Mid Craigie had one voice for everyone. I'm sure God liked that.

Hospital visiting was part of my work, and one day I had a surprise when I went into a ward. Out of the corner of my eye I saw a girl I used to drink with back home in Paisley. We had often given each other black eyes. Even though I was a Christian I'm ashamed to say that I walked past her. That night in my daily reading I came to the story of the Good Samaritan. God really spoke to me. He told me that I was like the priest and the Levite in the story; they too just walked past. God went on to show me that he had three words for me for every day of my life, and the words were STOP, LOOK and LISTEN. I went back to the hospital to visit the girl who was obviously very ill and needing to talk. It was a sordid story. When she was a child her mother had many 'uncles' coming to her home and she decided that when she grew up she would have a happy family life. She did until she lost her baby by a cot death and her husband left shortly afterwards. Her reaction was to build a wall around herself and not let anyone near. I didn't preach to her; I just shared my own experience of Jesus. She asked for a Bible and read the one I gave her. Things seemed to go well with her for a while then her cancer came back. I was with her when she heard that she only had weeks to live. She asked 'why?' then accepted it as God's will. My friend died on Easter morning with her Bible beside her, despite the fact that she had gone blind a short time before that. As I left church that morning I had a picture in my mind of my friend in Jesus' arm and her baby in his other arm. I was sad, but a song came into my mind and I sang it quietly as I walked home. 'Safe in the arms of Jesus, safe on his gentle breast, there by his love o'ershaded, sweetly my soul shall rest.' God used my friend to teach me to stop, look and listen, and I've tried to do that ever since.

Before I left Ferguslie Park I went with a group to Romania. Cammy was in the group too. I went back as often as I could after that, even from Dundee. Romania was very much in the news then after the terrible pictures of orphanages we saw on the television. We did outreach work there as well as practical things like cementing floors – I put my name and the date on a barn floor we cemented. One special time was spending a week working in a prison. As we left, the prisoners – there were about 1,000 of them – kissed my hand. While I was being kissed on one hand I handed them a pair of underpants with the other from the big stock I had of three different sizes. It is practical, down-to-earth things like that people need. Folk from

Paisley and Dundee came with me to Romania, and I was well known in Mid Craigie for going round the public houses with my Romanian collecting box. The Christian singer Ian White, was a great help with fundraising. Without him we would not have been able to do what we did. Both Ferguslie Park and Mid Craigie were poor areas and the people living there had very little for extras, but that didn't stop them wanting to help people worse off than themselves.

Among those who really supported me in my work in Dundee was Jock Stein, then minister of the Steeple Church in the city centre. He and his wife Margaret were always there for me, and they provided me with bigger tins of instant coffee than I knew existed!

Rev Jock Stein

May is an individualist; she doesn't fit into any mould. While she does her best to work within structures they always grate with her. She did have a good Management Team in Dundee and they worked together as well as any through some difficult times and situations. What May really needs is the liberty to use her God-given gifts in the ways she thinks best, and by and large the Christian world isn't quite ready for that yet. It took the people to whom May was responsible a little while to trust her enough to give her the freedom she needed. She would have gone on and done the work anyway, but it was good when her peculiar gifts began to be recognised and valued. And her gifts are peculiar. May can sniff out trouble from a mile away and be there in record time. Because she is utterly honest people are honest with her in return, and I'm sure she heard stories from folk's lives that nobody heard before or since.

One of the ministries Paul wrote about to the Ephesians was the ministry of evangelism. The Church of Scotland had for many years lay missionaries working in some areas, often quite difficult areas. They were more free agents than ministers, and tended to be evangelists. But over the years they became part of the institution, working in specific areas such as alcohol and drug rehabilitation. There were also deacons and deaconesses working in a serving ministry. Eventually these two amalgamated. Sadly the Church didn't recognise those with the gifts of an evangelist and find a role for them. I think there have been two outstanding evangelists in my time, Captain Stephen Anderson and May. Stephen Anderson did eventually find a place as a free-ranging evangelist, but the Church wasn't ready for May. However, God is bigger than one denomination and he has opened doors enabling May to use her gifts. The doors have opened in an interesting progression: first there was Paisley where May discovered her gifts and began to use them; then Mid Craigie where she developed before moving to Glasgow City Mission which established her back in the west coast and prepared the way for the work she is doing now, probably the first work that has really allowed her to use her gifts to the full.

10

Westward Ho!

Every Christian worker needs prayer support, and when I was working in Dundee a little group of ladies, who meet as the Candle Fellowship, took me under their wing. They are led by Amy Smith and they're real prayer warriors. When I'd been in Mid Craigie for about three years, Amy told me that she believed God was going to call me to work with Glasgow City Mission. I knew the work in Dundee was coming to an end but that was one move I certainly didn't expect. She was right and I was wrong. Rev Graeme Clark, then Executive Director of Glasgow City Mission, who knew about the work I was doing, contacted me and asked if I'd like to join them. While I'd been a missionary since the day I was converted this would

be the first time that title would be given to me
because I'd been an Outreach Worker in Ferguslie
Park and a Project Worker in Mid Craigie. The
thought of it took me right back to when I was a
girl at school listening to my RE teacher telling
us about the lives of missionaries. All those years
ago I'd decided that's what I wanted to be, now it
seemed as though that ambition might come true
after all.

Glasgow City Mission was looking for
someone to establish and run a rehabilitation
centre for girls who worked as prostitutes on the
city-centre streets. They didn't have premises but
were praying about it. The work with prostitutes
was to go ahead even if there was a delay in
finding a building. Although working with
prostitutes wasn't a major part of what I'd done
either in Paisley or Dundee I certainly had some
experience of it. There is no poor housing area
where some girls don't sell themselves, either to
buy food for their children or to keep themselves
in drugs. People often have totally wrong ideas
about prostitutes. They seem to think that they do
what they do because they like it. In all the years of
meeting women and girls who work the streets I've
never met one who did it for enjoyment. Usually
young girls are out there because they are addicted
to drugs and in desperation they sell themselves to
buy them. Sometimes a girl isn't an addict herself,
but she's living with a man who forces her to work
to fund his drug habit. And there are a few sad

girls who are on the streets because their parents have put them there. It's hard to believe these things happen, but life is brutally hard for some people. I thought all of this through, prayed about the move and discussed it with my friends, then decided that I should accept the job. Nine years after moving to Mid Craigie I was on the move again. When I started work with Glasgow City Mission things didn't turn out as I'd expected. City-centre work with prostitutes was not what I found myself doing. Instead I was sent to Govan to work in one of the Mission's Child and Family Centres, though I did go into Glasgow to work with girls on the streets one night a week. I knew in my own mind that God wanted me in Govan.

Maclain Service

My special responsibility as a Board member of Glasgow City Mission was for the Child and Family Centre in Govan. It was there I had the privilege of getting to know May and seeing her working first hand. She is a remarkable lady with unique abilities. May has the gift of making everyone she meets feel important and valued.

In some ways the area was different from anywhere I'd worked before. It's an old Victorian part of Glasgow, built up round shipbuilding. The buildings were mostly flats, many four or five storeys high. By the time I went there shipbuilding was almost a thing of the past, unemployment was high, and poverty and hardship were everywhere.

Common closes which once would have been sparkling clean were sometimes now filthy and smelling of urine. And polythene bags and empty glue and cigarette lighter fuel cans that sniffers had used littered some parts of Govan along with discarded needles. If ever an area needed a Family Centre this was it.

Those whom the Mission had put there already had their work cut out. Their job was to run a nursery. That sounds simple enough, but the mothers who came had so many problems that the workers had a choice – they could run a nursery for the children or they could try to help the mothers. They certainly needed someone else to come and work with them if both were to be done. I was appointed as an Adult Worker and immediately became involved with the mothers. Because I was there the girls who ran the nursery were able to do so much more effectively. They built it up to become an absolutely first-class preschool centre, and that's official. Its inspection report was great, which is not surprising as Anne Scott who runs it is a magnificent manager and a beautiful Christian. One of the points the inspector picked up was that the local mothers were very involved in running it for themselves. That was thanks to Anne's gift of encouragement.

I felt as though I was peeling an onion in more ways than one. When you go to a new area you only see the obvious problems; it takes time to peel off the layers of distrust and suspicion before you are accepted and get to the heart of things. That's what it was like for me. The other way it was like peeling an onion was that the things I saw and heard often made me want to cry. Much of the work in Govan turned out to be the same as I'd been doing before, but rather than repeat myself I'll tell it a bit differently. I'll mention some of the problems we met and try to explain what we tried to do about them.

Loneliness was a real problem, even for young mums. The only place some of them went was the Child and Family Centre, and the only real contact they had with people was with the others who went there. Because most of them had very little money to spare they weren't able to go out and socialise. That set the staff at the Centre thinking, and we decided that we'd try having an art class. At first it was mostly young mums who came, but soon older women began coming too. Only those who have been involved in a class like that can have any idea what it does for the people who go there. We did simple art and craft things to start with and one by one the women joined in. It was great to see them discovering what they could do and enjoying it. And because they were working with their hands they talked more to each other and to me. It's interesting, and I'd seen it before, but if people are just talking they sometimes avoid personal subjects because it's hard to look at a person and admit to feeling a failure. But if a group is working together that barrier breaks down and people share things they'd otherwise keep to themselves. We didn't call it art therapy, but that's what it was.

Even painting opened up ways of speaking about Jesus. When we did glass painting I remember using it as an illustration for the gospel. If you look at an unpainted glass you can see right through it and that's just like our lives without Jesus – there is nothing of substance there at all. But when he comes into our lives it's as though he paints beautiful things like joy, love and peace in us. I never preached, but I used every opportunity I had or could make to speak about Jesus. People didn't have to stay to listen; they were free to leave if they didn't like it, but nobody ever did.

One thing that was often talked about as they worked at craft things was poverty. When I was young in Ferguslie Park in the 1950s to be poor was to be really poor. The tragedy is that there are people today just as poor as we were then, especially young single mums. And we needn't get on to our high horses and say they shouldn't have got themselves into that situation. Girls don't set out to be single parents. They fall in love, or think they do, and the whole thing collapses around them, often leaving them with children to support. So as we talked about being poor the subject of credit unions came up and we encouraged the mums to use them. Credit unions are brilliant. Folk have to save in them regularly, even just 50p a week. Then when they've proved they can save they can borrow from the credit union and repay at an amount they can afford at very, very little interest. One of the shocking things about a place like Govan is that loan companies lend to people who are already in debt. I know girls who borrow from a loan company, then have to borrow from another one to pay the first one, then borrow from a third one to pay the second. And the interest they charge is criminal.

Another way we helped came out of hearing women talking about the price of school clothes. We suggested that they bring outgrown school clothes to the Centre and pass them on. Before long bags of children's clothes were arriving. Occasionally it was like Christmas with mums hunting through loads of children's clothes looking for something to fit their wee ones. There was no embarrassment in that situation; it was a laugh and they benefited from the laugh as well as from the clothes. A few of them might have been in tears otherwise.

Young mums were not the only folk in Govan who were lonely. There were many older people sitting looking out of their windows at life and not really taking part in it. That's why we started a lunch club. Apart from anything else it meant that those who came had one good meal in the day. They didn't eat their lunch then rush home again but stayed and enjoyed the company. When I heard about people on their own who didn't go out at all I used to visit them and encourage them to come to the lunch club. Some of them were scared to go out, and the longer they were on their own the worse that became. It took patience to encourage one or two people to come, but it was really worth it when they did and met friends they'd not seen for years. The conversations weren't all about old times; I often shared my testimony and it was great to see a number of those who came become Christians. When I was a young Christian it horrified me to think of people going to hell when they die, and I don't feel any different now. Old people may not have long to live but they still have eternity to come, and my heart just longs to see them becoming Christians before it's too late.

Among the pensioners that came were some from very sad situations, and we did our best to help. One lady, I'll call her Edith, was really upset. When I asked her what was wrong she told me that her son was schizophrenic and that he wasn't able to go out. He didn't have shoes or a jacket to his name. A night or two later I was speaking at a meeting and I asked if anyone had spare shoes, mentioning the size he needed. Before I left that night a woman from a shoe shop brought me some shoes and a man gave me a jacket. Edith was in tears when I took them to her. Not long afterwards she became a Christian; just a simple act of kindness had touched her heart. I was fond of Edith and really sad when she died. But I'll see her again in heaven.

For a while I spent one night a week in the city with girls who worked the streets. I remember one young prostitute in particular. When I told her I was terrified every time she went out on the streets she said that she'd be all right because the police had given her a rape alarm. Her story was the same one I'd heard over and over again. Abused as a wee girl, when she grew up she looked for someone who would really love her, only she chose someone who would send her out on the streets to earn money for his drug habit. She was told that if she didn't bring enough home each night her face would be smashed and she'd be unrecognisable in the morning. Why did she stay with him? She stayed because she was terrified what would happen if she left. After I'd prayed with that girl, she looked at me and said, 'May, I wish I'd had a mother like you.' I've never seen her since. Long ago I had to learn that I couldn't throw my arms round the whole world and keep it safe; I've got to let people go and leave them with the Lord. It wasn't easy, but I had to do it with that poor girl.

Part of my work was visiting alcoholics and drug addicts, and there were plenty of them. God was really good and some of the people I worked with were able to come off what they were addicted to. But that didn't always last. One girl I spent time with did really well, stopping drinking for months. It looked as though she was going to make it. Then one night she left her daughter with her mother and went out and took a drink. When she came home she sat down to relax with a cigarette and fell asleep. She was burned to death. A man I knew, a fine-looking big fellow, was told that if he didn't stop drinking he'd die. His liver was pickled. He tried really, really hard and managed to keep off it for two weeks. Then he started again and he did die. When things like that happen they break my heart. I'll never get used to them.

Often it was the families of alcoholics and drug addicts that I was able to support. They go through terrible times; I know that from what Mum went through with me. And their children don't always survive. One girl I knew was a drug addict, taking both heroin and jellies (Temazepam capsules opened and the stuff inside injected). She was in prison and when she came out she took the same dose of both as she'd been taking before she went in. It killed her. It nearly killed her family too because, like my mum, they still had hopes for her; they still believed she might come off drugs and recover.

We worked with one man in Govan whose two daughters were addicts. He put them out of the house as they were selling everything they could get their hands on to feed their habit. Life was a living hell for him. I once asked him how he coped. 'I don't cope,' he said. 'I just live from day to day wondering when the next addict I know will die.' What young addicts don't realise is that there are no old drug addicts; they either kick the habit or it kicks them. That man's two daughters died. I prayed with him and shared my faith with him. And I also put him in touch with a local group that supports families who've lost children to drugs.

Addiction to anything is a problem, and I believe that there is such a thing as an addictive personality. That's what I have. I'm not making excuses for having been an alcoholic, but I still believe it's a fact. Since the day I stopped drinking I've never craved drink and I thank God for that. But I could let myself become addicted to other things. When I was drinking, if I had a drink I needed another, then another. There have been times when I've made a nice birthday card and I've had an urge to go on making them, one after another. I have to watch that, even if what I'm doing is absolutely wholesome, I won't let it take me over, or take over my time. If I let myself, I could become addicted to old films! I'm glad God left me with an addictive personality because it never allows me to forget what it's like. If a craving for drink ever did hit me I'd phone a friend right away. I've had to do that with other temptations in the past because I'd rather humble myself and ask a friend for support than fall into serious sin. I've seen that too often, even with Christian leaders. Sometimes God reminds me of the time I wasn't reading my Bible and it was stuffed underneath all the newspapers. If we take our eyes off Jesus our lives just fill up with junk. In a strange way the fact that I was a notorious drunk has turned out to be a kind of protection. Because people watch what I do I'm careful. God sees me all the time too.

For two summers during the nine years I worked with Glasgow City Mission a man kindly lent me his house in St Andrews. We could have filled it ten times over with people who needed a holiday. I don't think my dad and mum had a holiday until I was fourteen years old, and there are many people today just like them. Young families who went to St Andrews had the kind of holiday folk used to have 30 years ago. It didn't cost them much because the children were happy to play in the sand and paddle in the sea. And older people went too and relaxed in a way they couldn't do at home. The pressure was off and they just enjoyed themselves. Even Jesus needed time away.

While I was working in Govan things were not so good on the home front. The part of Paisley I lived in was nicknamed 'Little Bosnia' because that's just what it looked like. One night 32 car windows were smashed and there were reports of groups running around the area carrying machetes. Although I loved my house I didn't feel safe, especially when my grandchildren stayed with me. One day I was sitting on the bus going home when I saw a really nice house that looked empty. Turning to the woman next to me, I said, 'I wish I could afford to buy that wee house.' 'You can't,' she replied. 'That's a council house.' So I went to the Council and asked if there was any possibility of me renting it and was told that there was a list as long as my arm waiting for it. But every time I passed it still looked empty. I decided to phone the Council and learned that the person who had been offered it hadn't taken it. The house was to be offered to someone else. Several people were offered it and none took it. Ever hopeful, I phoned over and over again and eventually I was offered it. I was so delighted that I accepted the house without seeing the inside. When I got the key and went to look at it my heart sank. It needed to be gutted.

The Council wouldn't do the work and I hadn't a penny in the bank, not one single penny. I sat on the wall at the back of the house and cried. God spoke to my heart, telling me that my life used to be just like that house. It was run down; it was rubbish. And what did he do? I told the Lord that he had taken my life and filled it with beautiful things. Suddenly I knew that he was going to make that wee house a place of love where people would come to feel loved; a house of laughter where sad people would feel happy; a house of healing for people who were hurt; and a house where people would come to know him. So I went into the house with a vision, but it was hard to see how it would ever be liveable in, far less be used for all these wonderful things.

Because I thought I'd no other choice I went into the bank and applied for a bank loan. But before the money came through my friend Amy Smith phoned and told me she'd been picturing my house. 'I imagined that God had a big basket above it,' she said. 'It was filled with streamers and gifts and they were all going down into your house.' That was a real rebuke. God didn't need a bank loan to provide for me and I went in to cancel it. When the girl in the bank asked how I was going to get the money I needed, I told her that I didn't know but that God would provide for me. And he did. I was given a bathroom suite, curtains, blinds, tiles for the bathroom and kitchen, carpeting, light shades, kitchen units, a fireplace and fire, and money that paid for everything else I needed. I didn't ask for a single one of them, and some gifts were given by people I hardly knew. Not only that, God even provided labourers to do all the jobs that needed done. The whole house was refurbished and I wasn't a penny in debt. And God is using my home just as I knew he would. It is a house of love and laughter and healing, and people have met Jesus in it.

11

Another New Beginning

My work with Glasgow City Mission in Govan lasted for nine years, then circumstances showed me that it was God's time for me to leave. I believed he still wanted me in Govan, but the Mission's work was about to change and in order to continue doing what I was doing I had to branch out on my own. It was an act of faith that I've not regretted once. The Christian singer Ian White, was a great support to me then. He had faced the same kind of decision before he took the step of faith and became a professional singer. Ian was convinced of what I should do. 'Step out in faith, May,' he said. 'God is really going to bless this work, not just in Govan but in other places too.' My work finished with the Mission on the last Friday of June 2002 and the following Monday a new work began based in a local Church of Scotland hall. Rev David Keddie saw the value of what we were doing and his congregation agreed to us using their premises until we found our own. Before long we were established as the Preshal Trust. Preshal is Gaelic for 'precious', and our stated aim is that we are 'caring for families, valuing people and providing spiritual and practical care'. To put it another way, we try to show folk that they are precious to us and even more precious to God. Basically I was going to be doing exactly what I'd been doing before, but being an independent trust meant that we could respond to needs as we met them and expand.

When Preshal was established MacIain Service became our Chairman – it was his wife Jo who suggested the name Preshal – and the Duchess of Montrose was appointed President. Neither of them is just involved in name; both help hands-on when they can, and that's true of the other Trustees too. Our initial expenses were covered by a grant from Greater Govan Social Inclusion Partnership which gave us enough to employ me full time, and four others part-time: Rena is our administrator, Irene is a project worker, Eleanor and Kim use their skills in a variety of ways.

MacIain Service

A Chinese philosopher said, 'A journey of a thousand miles begins with the first step', and we took that step in faith. What is the journey? Our big vision is that we should help to set up groups like the Preshal Trust wherever there is a need. May is a first-class team builder and excellent leader. She has already established a great team in Govan, one that will continue to expand the work there, work that is already being used as a prototype by groups in other areas. I esteem it an honour and a privilege to be working closely with May in the Preshal Trust, where her great gifts are flourishing and benefiting and blessing an increasing number of people.

Being involved in Preshal is wonderful. People think that we are here to help the people of Govan; they don't realise how much the people of Govan do for us. We are loved and accepted and treated as real friends, and we all learn together. That's a privilege. What amazes me is that there's so much talent in people just waiting to be discovered. In fact, Preshal is a process of discovery for us all. Although it started off with the women I knew from the Family and Child Centre it wasn't long before men started coming too. God was great. He provided money to pay a man to work with the men. Alex is with Preshal part-time and he does a power of work. In Spring 2003 we discovered that there was a suitable building we could rent just minutes away from the church hall! We moved in and have now settled down there.

We are open every morning from Monday to Friday and we hope to expand beyond that. Monday is our arts and crafts day. We started the art group right away and it's a great success. We do card making, glass painting, pin craft, decoupage and many other things as well. Two of our workers and one volunteer have already been on courses to learn more craft work. When people first come to Preshal they sometimes sit at the side and say that they can't do the arts and crafts. But usually they join in eventually and some of them have discovered they have gifts they didn't know anything about, and their self-confidence and self-esteem have improved amazingly. Workers have gone on other courses too. All are now trained in First Aid, some in Health and Safety, Steps to Excellence, Stress Management, and they have done the MIDAS course in driving the minibus for the disabled. On-going educational training will be a feature of our work, hopefully in the afternoons. We also run a saving scheme, with both money and shop's saving stamps, that allows people to save as little as a pound a week for Christmas. Little things like that make a big difference if they help young mums to stay out of debt. On Tuesdays we serve breakfast then have our pensioners' morning with quizzes, beetle drives, etc. There's often karaoke that day. It's so popular that most people want to sing. It doesn't matter if they are good singers or not because everyone joins in. We make things with our pensioners too: sweets, candles, table decorations, fridge magnets and the like. Before we leave on Tuesdays someone gives a testimony to what God has done in his or her life. People really listen because they are full of human interest. Sometimes we take our pensioners for trips. Last Christmas we went by minibus to Auchtermuchty where there was an outdoor nativity play with real animals and shepherds actually coming down a hillside! The tickets were expensive but we were given them as a gift. The Countess of Dundee gave us our tea in her own home before we went to the play. She treated us like queens, and that really was a treat for my ladies from Govan! Another weekend I went with some of our pensioners to Eredine, a beautiful conference centre in Argyll. That's where I met Irene who has written my story; she was the speaker. One Govan lady became a Christian that weekend and she is still walking with the Lord. Candle Fellowship paid for us to go to Eredine. The Fellowship doesn't just support us in prayer but in practical ways too.

Wednesday is a drop-in day and very informal. Sometimes folk bring in forms they need help with or discuss practical things with a member of staff. A lot happens on Wednesdays. We have our line-dancing for which a tutor was arranged free of charge through the local Community Learning Flat. Young and old join in together and it's great fun as well as good exercise. There might be one-to-one reading with someone who missed out on learning to read at school, counselling, or arrangements made to meet the different social work agencies or even a lawyer. Many people don't know how to access the help they need and the staff are there to point them in the right direction. On Wednesday afternoons I try to visit anyone who didn't turn up to the pensioners' morning in case they need help. We visit women in ones because we know the people, but in twos when we're going to a man. The Bible says that we should, 'Abstain from all appearance of evil' (1 Thessalonians 5:22 AV) and it's really important we do that. The last thing we need is for Preshal to get a bad name in the area. Our folk often tell us about people they are worried about and ask us to visit. We do that, and try to befriend them before inviting them to Preshal. We also visit folk in hospital, those we know and others we hear about. Sometimes we attend tribunals, etc., with people who want our support.

A mixture of things happen on Thursdays: painting, drawing, picture framing (some of our young women have been trained to do that), and the men have pool and domino tournaments as well as visits to local places of interest. We also have a short Bible study for those who want to find out more about the Lord. Up to twenty come along. Some of those who come are seeking, and others are new Christians. Mary Scott, who is one of our volunteers, usually takes it and occasionally we have someone in to give a short talk. We finish with prayer and people say what they specially want prayed for. When Nancy was converted she told me after the meeting had ended that she would have loved to pray aloud but was too nervous. She said she was going home to practise. 'Just pray what's in your heart,' I told her. She did. Nancy prayed a beautiful simple prayer thanking God that she had Preshal to go to and for all the new friends she had made there.

Nancy

I had six children but one of them died as a baby. After the baby died the doctor told me to get down on my knees and thank God for taking him because I wouldn't have been able to cope. He would only have lived for about three years. My husband was an alcoholic who died when he was 59. I worked as a railway cleaner for twenty years then I had another job until past retirement age. It was hard work. But May brought me here and I do work I'm more able for. My children are grown up and they're doing their best. I'm really proud of them. May took me to a meeting one night and I listened to what she said about Jesus and became a Christian. That was about three years ago. Life is totally different now. Jesus has changed my life and I've even stood up and given my testimony at a meeting! I was very nervous but God helped me.

SANDRA (Nancy's daughter)

Mum is happier now than I've ever known her. She just loves getting up in the morning and going to Preshal. I met my husband when I was eighteen. He was murdered nearly three years ago, stabbed 29 times in a pub. I'm bringing up my daughters on my own now. Mum helped me a lot when my man died, and it was through Mum that I met May. She has helped me such a lot, talking to me and praying with me and for the girls. I see her as my friend. We're all friends with each other here. May loves us all. I'll never be able to thank her for what she did for Mum.

Each Friday morning a variety of activities take place and we have our staff meeting. That is so important. We discuss the week and evaluate what has been done. Where we recognise that things could have been better we try to work out how to improve them. Then we plan for the following week. Although Preshal looks informal it is actually carefully planned. If it weren't planned there would be chaos. That doesn't mean that we can't be flexible and respond to the people who come in. The team time is valuable too because we can work out any little niggles before they become big problems. Even Christians don't always agree about things, but if they are dealt with right at the very beginning it avoids problems in the future. The team at Preshal is great and really does work together. We only have to look at the people who come in to know that God is blessing what we do.

Libby

My brother was murdered when he was four. I was six, and when he died I had to become a mother and look after Mum. When I was grown up and married, Mum got cancer. I looked after her and she died in my arms when she was 52. I miss her terribly. After that my father, best friend and partner all died. I stayed in the house for three years and wouldn't even go down the stairs. I asked God to help me and all of a sudden my life changed. Since I started coming to Preshal it still hurts, but not so much. I come here because I'm among people who care. May has done more for me than anyone else in my life. That's what makes her special to me.

(Libby runs our fruit and vegetable co-op on a Thursday morning. Many Govan children would never have really fresh fruit and vegetables without this – and they love trying exotic fruits too!)

Sandra

I used to dread each day. Before I started coming here I didn't want to wake up in the morning and I used to live all day for bedtime. There are lots of people here who care, whoever you are and whatever's wrong with you. It's OK to come here. There's peace here.

Other things happen in the afternoons. For example, we've sent people to the Linthouse Community Learning Flat to do Information Technology courses, and it wasn't just the young ones who went. One older woman did the course because she has family abroad and wants to be able to e-mail them. Courses run at the Flat are free and we make good use of them. We hope to have upholstery classes in the future. While the women are busy, Alex does other activities with the men. They get out and about too. Some even spent a weekend walking the West Highland Way, nearly 100 miles of it!

Michael

I was on a detox course when I first came here and if it hadn't been for this place I couldn't have done it. It's been great for me. I was in children's homes and one thing led to another. I started taking heroin when someone tried it in the house. A few days later I thought I had a cold but it was withdrawals so I took more. That week turned into years and it all spiralled. I've lived with my partner all over Glasgow, then we came to Govan. That's when I noticed this place and saw May at the door. I feel safe here. Sometimes I find it hard to accept the kindness. I've never been able to do things for nice people before. Someone gave me a bike for nothing and I've been going cycling with my daughter Shirley. May's dead easy to approach. I've not known her for long but I could talk to her about anything. Shirley and my partner love her too. She comes to visit us at home. My partner is going to come soon though she's not been going out. May is helping her. I think May reminds me of Jesus.

(Michael is now at college doing a Care course. He still comes to Preshal on his days off).

Many of the people who come to Preshal have problems, but they are our friends. There isn't a line between staff and those who come. We're all helping each other. And because people feel involved they still keep coming. That's certainly true of George and Betty. I've known them for many years and they come faithfully to the project and are a great help.

George and Betty

George – *I met May in a wee mission hall about twelve years ago. I was an alcoholic. May said I should bring my wife. I went home and told Betty that May wanted to see her.*

Betty – *I went with George and met May. She really made me feel at ease and she asked if I'd like to help out. I've been coming ever since. That's how May gets people involved; she asks them to be volunteers and that keeps them coming.*

George – *Once when I'd been off the drink for three months I went to the pub one day and bought a can of lager. Then I looked around me and saw all these folk with black eyes and stitches in their faces. I thought to myself, that's what I look like when I'm drunk. So I gave the drink back to the barman and told him to pour it down the plughole. I've not looked back and that's thanks to May's support.*

Betty – *When George was drinking he had terrible moods. He used to break things about the house and throw eggs and things. I was scared to go out of the house, not because of his drinking, just the area we lived in. George calmed down when he came off the drink. I've known May all these years and I suppose I treat her like a mum. I can speak to her. She's always a good help, and she gave me support when nobody else would. Our four girls call May 'Mammy'.*

George – *I was so bad with the drinking that I was in a wheelchair. All my nerves were damaged and my liver as well. That's how bad I was. I'm still nervy. This place helps me a lot. I live for coming here.*

I am often invited to speak at churches and other groups. People are always interested in the work and want to know how they can help. Many support us financially, but I always ask them to hand in clothes and basic shopping to the project. Bags of clothes are donated regularly, and on Fridays one of the jobs the staff does is sort them out. We fill black bags with a selection of clothes, basic foods like cereals, soup, beans, tea bags and porridge, then we add a treat like chocolate biscuits or sweets, and a power card. It's amazing how often when we give these bags out people have nearly nothing. They can be the difference between children going to bed hungry and going to bed fed. Many churches and individuals support us and I could write a whole book about that! It was when I was speaking at a

Guild meeting that I first met Preshal's President, the Duchess of Montrose, but she'll tell her own story later. I've also spoken at churches that are interested in setting up a family support scheme in their own area.

I don't believe in coincidences. When we give a bag of food and clothes to someone who really needs it God arranged it that way. One day we had a great example of his perfect arrangements. Some asylum seekers who were placed in the area saw Preshal's open door and came in, eight or nine families in all. We helped them with the different agencies that they find so confusing. One young mother brought her eight-week-old baby all dressed in pink. 'What a lovely wee girl,' I said. But it was a boy, and pink clothes were all she had. We found some clothes for her baby and she was delighted. That mum carried her baby everywhere because she didn't have a pram. When I realised that I contacted our mothers and they spread the word until a pram was found. She was thrilled. One day an asylum seeker from the Congo came in. She could only speak French. The Duchess of Montrose was in that day and she was able to speak French with her. God organised that! I felt really sorry for these asylum seekers because things weren't easy for them. One family had been farmers in their own country and they were placed in the top flat of a four-storey building. The children were used to running free and they ran up and down the stairs instead. One of their downstairs neighbours came out and punched their father. They had a much warmer welcome than that at Preshal.

Christmas is a time for warmth and happiness, and at the end of our first year of Preshal we wondered what to do for Christmas that would be special. We decided to make cards. Just then a friend phoned to say that a group from America was coming to Edinburgh to do a mission. I asked if they had time to run an outreach in Govan. They had – and they used card craft as an introduction to giving their testimonies! Our people were delighted. Many of them were in tears as they listened to the difference Jesus had made in the mission team's lives. Before they left the Americans donated hundreds of pounds worth of craft material to Preshal.

The day before Christmas a woman phoned me. She had been placed in Govan by the social services after fleeing to Scotland from Northern Ireland to escape an abusive relationship. There was hardly a thing in her house, not even carpets on the floors or enough beds for her ten children. But that didn't bother her; there was such a sense of relief and happiness in their home. What did bother the woman was that she had nothing for her children's Christmas, and someone she'd met told her about Preshal. Everyone rallied round and that night a whole pile of toys, selection boxes and food was delivered. I called in the following day to wish them a happy Christmas … and they were certainly having one! The children literally jumped for joy. 'God sent us to you,' their mum said. That's what

Preshal is all about, putting our faith into action as well as words. That was a last minute Christmas treat, but we'd been organising other things for weeks. As well as having a party for our folk, we made up Christmas boxes for children who would otherwise have had very little, and food parcels for their mums – all with some treats in them too. Seagate Evangelical Church funded the whole thing and did the same the following year. Many churches support Preshal in very special ways.

Not everyone is at home for Christmas, or for the rest of the year either. Among the people who come to Preshal are ex-offenders and we try to support them as they rebuild their lives. But we hope to become much more involved with prisoners than that. Alex and I were speaking in a prison one day when a boy approached us who was being released the following morning. We told him about the project and he and his partner came along. We were there for them when they needed us. A meeting has already been held with the Governor of Corntonvale Prison and Social Inclusion and we hope that's an area that will develop soon. Of course, it would be better still to meet young people before they offend in the first place and we're also working on that. Roy Lees and Bill Kerr, who gave me Joseph my multicoloured estate car, are involved with Teen Challenge, and they have given us a bus to use one night a week. We are just about to begin work with it. Parked in the centre of Govan it will attract the local young people in the same way that the caravan did in Mid Craigie. Among those who come will be many with addiction problems – they make up the biggest proportion of young offenders – and we'll be able to refer them on to Teen Challenge that has its own rehabilitation centre. Preshal is not just about picking up the pieces when something is broken; it's about stopping it breaking in the first place.

12

Sisters in the Lord

I was invited to speak at a Guild about the work I was doing in Govan. After I'd given my talk I went to chat with the women who were there. I'm not one for sitting at the front having tea with the Chairman! One lady was especially interested and she and I got on well together. As she knew about me from my talk, I asked her about herself. She told me how she became a Christian, but I felt she was shy of witnessing to Jesus. I said that to her. 'I know you're right,' she replied, 'but I'm frightened of putting people off.' From what the woman had told me I knew that folk would be interested in her story, and I encouraged her to share her testimony more often. So many Christians have wonderful experiences of Jesus but they keep them all to themselves. It wasn't until later in the evening that someone told me that the woman who had introduced herself to me as Cathy Montrose was actually the Duchess of Montrose. Cathy was so interested in the work in Govan that she became involved with Preshal right at the very beginning and she is now our President.

Christians come from different kinds of backgrounds but they are all just the same; every one of them is a sinner saved by God's grace. A humble old lady in Govan and a duchess are sisters if they have the same Father in heaven. But we are so used to looking at things differently that it does the humble folk in Govan good when a duchess is one of their friends, and it does her good too when they befriend her. Preshal is all about building real friendships, two-way friendships, and Cathy is a very real part of that.

Catherine Montrose

Meeting May at the Guild really made me think. I was used to doing charity fundraising work, but giving my personal testimony is very different. Because I was concerned about offending people, or putting them off, I was hesitant to be that personal. May's words really challenged me and in a way they changed my life. Before very long she had me doing things to support the work – I now recognise that is how May gets people involved! I enjoyed going to Govan and felt I could help there, though I never thought of public speaking. That was until May invited me to join her at a meeting of the Candle Fellowship. We were at the meeting before I really grasped that we were both expected to speak! I was so nervous. 'You're speaking first,' May said. 'No, you speak first then I can fill in the gaps', I protested, and that is what happened. May did that quite deliberately as she wanted me to speak from my heart rather than put my security in pages of written notes. That experience gave my faith a boost. If you trust in the Lord he really will help you. We have spoken together at quite a number of meetings since then, and doing that has allowed me to be more relaxed when I am speaking to individuals too.

I believe God has brought May and me together because he has work for us to do. However, he has taken us along very different roads to get here. Although I was born in Canada, the youngest of four children, my family had previously lived in the Gold Coast where my father lectured at Achimota College. They moved back to my parents' homeland of Canada where Father founded a boys' school in Winnipeg before going to fight in the Second World War. He was killed in 1942 in the Dieppe Raid. I was six years old. Although I have a few memories of life with my father, like sitting on his shoulders when the King and Queen passed through Winnipeg, they are very few. I was not at home when the news came of Father's death, but when I next saw my mother she was absolutely radiant. She had had an experience of God. When I saw her face I remember thinking that things would be all right; she gave me such a sense of security. The one place that Mother wept was in church and that made me not want to go there, although I did attend because I was expected to.

When I was a teenager and a student I went with Mother to Britain. She travelled on from there to Ghana and we arranged to meet up at a conference in Switzerland. I had ten days there before Mother arrived and that gave me the opportunity to listen to what people were saying. I was looking for meaning in life. I think I was still hurting badly from losing my father when I was such a small child, and that had affected my relationship with Mother. One night I enjoyed a meal with a very pleasant couple. 'How old are you?' the gentleman asked. I told him I was eighteen. He thought for a moment before replying. 'If I were eighteen, and had a chance not to make the same mistakes again, I would put my trust in Jesus.' What he said set me thinking. I decided that if there was a God I would ask him to tell me what I should do with my life. Thinking I would be given earth-shaking guidance I was taken aback when I was led to apologise to my sister for being jealous and superior because she was not at university, and to be honest with my mother. When I did speak to Mother she said that she recognised that she had given me education and security but had missed out on the most important thing of all which was helping me to find a faith, though I do believe she sowed the seeds of my faith. I was touched by her humility, and the barriers that had built up between us over the years came down.

My life until then had been self-centred, but I began to ask God each day what he wanted me to do. He showed me all kinds of things and began to be very much a part of my life and thinking. The following summer was spent travelling on three different continents. I learned many things as I travelled, among them that while God guides you, you have to discipline your life. That involves prayer, Bible reading, noting what God teaches you and doing what he prompts you to do. I found God led me to like-minded people, and he still does. That is how I met May. There is no place for someone from my background being superior. We all need God; we are level and equal, and all equally need forgiveness.

I had met Seumas from time to time as our paths crossed, but I did not think I meant anything to him. We *both travelled a great deal and had friends in common. On one trip back to Europe I discovered that he had told mutual friends that he cared about me. They arranged for us to have a meal with them, then left us on our own together! I am grateful to them because we have now been happily married for 33 years. That was such a lesson to me. God gave me gifts beyond my wildest dreams in Seumas, our three children and two grandchildren. At that time he was the Marquis of Graham and we made our home in Scotland where he was a working farmer. Even when we first came I never felt lonely; God always had something for me to do. When his father died Seumas became the Duke of Montrose and he sits in the House of Lords. Although I am never lonely, I always feel just a little sad when he leaves on Mondays for London, even though I know he will be home in a few days time.*

We are very involved in our local Church of Scotland, and it was at a Guild meeting there that I met May for the first time. She was then with Glasgow City Mission and she told us about her work. May and I found ourselves sitting together for tea and, although I do not speak much about myself, before I knew what I was doing I had embarked on my life story! That is what happens when you sit next to May. She loves people, and she has a passion to do what God wants her to do and to win souls for him. Through God's grace she is a real life-changer. I am trying to be more open and frank about what I believe and to search for ways of reaching out to people. But it is God who changes lives, and I have to leave the results in his hands.

Before long I was involved in the work May was doing, and when she took the step of faith to leave the Mission and form an independent trust I was keen to be involved. It is my privilege to be President of the Preshal Trust. Right from the beginning Preshal went from strength to strength.

Every time I went to Govan, or heard a report about what was happening, there were things to encourage and rejoice over, which was why May's illness in the early summer of 2003 took us all by surprise. It seemed strange that God was allowing her to suffer from cancer just when the work was being established. But he does not make mistakes, and we look forward to seeing how he uses this time of illness as a blessing. He will do that.

If anyone had told me before I was converted how my life would turn out, I would have laughed until I couldn't laugh any more. I was a no-hoper; my life was worth nothing. The truth is that if I hadn't stopped drinking I would have died long ago. When I look back at old photos I can see that I look younger now than I did when I was 25 years old. And if someone had suggested that I'd visit a duchess's home I would have thought it was the name of a pub. Now Cathy is as much a friend to me as the people I meet down in Govan. She even organised my birthday tea. Mum would have loved that!

The vision behind Preshal is that when it is established in Govan a team will be left there to carry on the work and I'll move to another place and set up another centre, then another, until there is a whole network. The original Govan team: Rena Feeney, Irene McGregor, Eleanor McLaughlin and Kim Scott, was ideal for the job, and with the addition of Alex McMillan the work with men fitted in nicely. Within a few months I could envisage a time coming when they would continue the work in Govan and release me to move on. Then at the beginning of June 2003 I discovered a lump, and a week later I was told that I had breast cancer. As I left the hospital that day with my friend Cheryl, I remembered that I'd been able to reach out to alcoholics because I was once where they are now, and I realised that I'd now be able to reach out to people with cancer and say, 'I understand. I've got cancer too.' My approach at that time was: this week I have cancer, next week I'll have surgery and then it's all over except the treatment.

Right from the beginning I was told that the outlook for me was very good, that the cancer didn't seem to have spread. Chemotherapy treatments began to fill my diary rather than speaking engagements, and radiotherapy was pencilled in too. This book is being finished three-quarters way through my treatment and things are going very well. I've discovered a new meaning of the expression 'a bad hair day' – it's when someone gives me such a big cuddle that my wig nearly falls off!

One place where the cuddles are very enthusiastic is Northern Ireland, and I was able to go over for a weekend not long after I discovered I had cancer. I first went to Belfast's Bogside two years ago with a friend, and we met some lovely Christians. We had such a laugh one day when we went into an inn and asked if they did lunches. The man pointed to a table. 'There's the Pot Noodles and there's the kettle. Help yourself!' They are my kind of people! The community isn't very different from Govan or Mid Craigie or Ferguslie Park as the social problems are exactly the same, though sectarianism is even worse there than in Glasgow. I've been over often since then and love going to their fellowship that straddles the sectarian divide. It's only interested in being Christian. Groups from Preshal visit the Bogside, and folk from there come here. We've built up a relationship that's good for both places and I know my friends there are praying for me, for my treatment and for Preshal too. They've even come over to see how I'm doing.

God doesn't make any mistakes, and he knew what he was doing when he gave Preshal the team it has to do the practical work at the centre. And the best set of Trustees in the world (that's what I tell them!) look after the business side of things as well as helping in other ways. They are Catherine Montrose (President), MacIain Service (Chairman), Rev David Keddie (Secretary), William Storm (Treasurer), Ina Munro, Brett Nicholls, Gavin Shanks, Jim and Noreen MacFarlane and Brian McLaughlin. For the last few weeks I've had to stay away from the centre altogether in case I catch an infection, but things are running just as smoothly without me. That's a terrific encouragement. It brings moving Preshal into other areas one step nearer. I'm looking forward to being back at work full-time before too long but I'm happy to leave Preshal in God's hands.

One of the things about being a Christian is that you are never pensioned-off or given sick leave. However old or ill you are God still has work for you to do. If you're in an old people's home or hospital he wants you to shine like a star right where you are. Being in hospital for my operation, and now going back and forward for treatment, has given me some great opportunities to tell people what Jesus has done in my life. And they often bring up the subject because when you're facing death in the eye there's no point in pretending. I think women are better at that kind of honesty than men.

The day before my chemotherapy I have blood taken, and if the tests show that it is all right I go ahead and have my treatment. I've lost a lot of blood that way! When the nurses take my blood they can't help seeing the slash marks on my arms, and that gives me the opportunity to tell them about my life as a suicidal alcoholic and how Jesus saved me out of it. One day someone came for the nurse when I was halfway through my story, she said she'd be along in a minute or two because she wanted to hear the rest of it. Having cancer has allowed me to give my testimony to doctors and nurses I'd never have met otherwise. Some of them are Christians, and maybe one day others will be too if God uses what they've heard to make them think.

What came into my mind the day I heard I had cancer has turned out to be true. I can talk to other patients about Jesus because we have something in common. We understand what we're each going through. Having chemotherapy isn't nice, and it brings all kinds of little problems that we can talk about when we're sitting around together. But the biggest problem of all is facing death without Jesus, and I've been able to talk to some of them about him. More often though it's just a case of telling people that I'm a Christian and that I'll pray for them. That's just a few words, but I can tell from their responses that it means a lot.

I'm a doer, in fact I'm a non-stop doer, and I've had to learn to slow down and sometimes to stop. That's been a bit of a steep learning curve. But the ones who have made it possible are Tracey and Alan. They've been brilliant and I'm really, really proud of them. They both have busy lives with their families and their work but they could not do more for me. When I think back to the kind of mother I was to them both when they were little, I know cancer is letting me see once again that God is keeping the promise he made to me when I was converted. Without me even knowing they came from the Bible, God gave me the words, 'I will restore to you the years the locusts have eaten' (Joel 2:25). I started drinking when I was fifteen years old, and the locusts of drink, drugs and self-harming ate 19 years of my life. I've had 23 wonderful years since then, and I've seen both

Tracey and Alan become Christians. I don't know how many more years I have to live but I'm content to leave that in God's hands. He's done brilliantly so far, and he's not going to make any mistakes in the future. And the best is still to come when I see Jesus.

Anyone wishing further information about the Preshal Trust should contact:

preshaltrust@hotmail.com
Tel: 0141 445 3689
PO Box 7344
8 Aboukir Street
Glasgow
G51 4QX

more
MIRACLES *from* MAYHEM

The continuing story of May Nicholson and the Preshal Trust

IRENE HOWAT

More Miracles from Mayhem

The continuing story of May Nicholson and the Preshal Trust

Irene Howat

In *Miracles from Mayhem* May Nicholson told the story of how she went from being a drunk no-hoper to establishing Preshal, a Christian trust based in one of the most needy areas of Glasgow. Preshal comes from the Gaelic word for precious, and Preshal aims to show those who come in that they are precious, whatever their circumstances, whatever their needs, whatever their addictions, whatever the state of their mental health. Opening *More Miracles from Mayhem* opens the door to Preshal and allows the reader to meet those who come through the door, both locals seeking friendship and support as well as members of the staff, several of whom have come up through the ranks.

Those who tell their stories in *More Miracles from Mayhem* come from all sorts of backgrounds, from loving and Christian homes through to abusive and manipulative backgrounds to having no home at all, rather spending over 30 years in the care system. The book will move readers to tears, to laughter and to prayer. This book will give you new hope as you read of those who have come through terrible times and have found faith and hope.

ISBN 978-1-84550-449-6

IRENE HOWAT & MAY NICHOLSON

RENEWING
BROKEN
LIVES

Even More Miracles
from Mayhem

Renewing Broken Lives
Even More Miracles from Mayhem
Irene Howat and May Nicholson

May Nicholson's story, told so powerfully in *Miracles from Mayhem* and *More Miracles from Mayhem*, tells of how she went from being a drunk no-hoper to establishing Preshal, a Christian trust based in one of the most needy areas of Glasgow. The work of Preshal and its impact continue to challenge and inspire. In *Renewing Broken Lives* you will find May's story and the story of Preshal interwoven with the stories that men and women tell of their own lives. The book will be sure to move readers to tears, to laughter and to prayer.

ISBN 978-1-78191-685-8

Christian Focus Publications

Our mission statement –

STAYING FAITHFUL

In dependence upon God we seek to impact the world through literature faithful to His infallible Word, the Bible. Our aim is to ensure that the Lord Jesus Christ is presented as the only hope to obtain forgiveness of sin, live a useful life and look forward to heaven with Him.

Our books are published in four imprints:

CHRISTIAN
FOCUS

Popular works including biographies, commentaries, basic doc-trine and Christian living.

CHRISTIAN
HERITAGE

Books representing some of the best material from the rich heritage of the church.

MENTOR

Books written at a level suitable for Bible College and seminary students, pastors, and other serious readers. The imprint includes commentaries, doctrinal studies, examination of current issues and church history.

CF4•K

Children's books for quality Bible teaching and for all age groups: Sunday school curriculum, puzzle and activity books; personal and family devotional titles, biographies and inspirational stories – because you are never too young to know Jesus!

Christian Focus Publications Ltd,
Geanies House, Fearn, Ross-shire,
IV20 1TW, Scotland, United Kingdom.
www.christianfocus.com